Dog Traini
Instructor's

C000231141

by Angela White

For Life

Gilpa has successfully fed generations of dogs, keeping them in peak condition. Knowing that all dogs are different, Gilpa has developed a range of complete foods that provide a balanced feeding regime for all shapes and sizes. Easy to feed and good to eat, Gilpa provides a nutritionally balanced diet, keeping dogs healthy and sustaining energy levels throughout their life.

For more information please contact our Customer Services Hotline on: 01707 367909

Guaranteed Premium Nutrition at a Sensible Price.

formulated for life

Gilbertson & Page,
PO Box 321, Welwyn Garden City, Herts AL7 1LF Tel: 01707 367900 Fax: 01707 339221

Guaranteed Premium Nutrition at a Sensible Price.

Guaranteed Premium Nutrition at a Sensible Price is the powerful commitment that **Gilbertson & Page Ltd.,** has made with their **Gilpa Pet Food Range** to each and every dog owner.

Premium nutrition means that **Gilpa Pet Foods** is entrusted with selecting the most up to date, effective and innovative nutrition, thus guaranteeing that all the requirements, well being and quality of life of your dog will be enhanced and ensured.

Sensible price is achieved through carefully chosen, quality assured, consistent and recognisable ingredients from approved suppliers who seek to partner **Gilpa** in this campaign. Ingredients are selected, in addition to their overall quality, for the contribution that each and every nutrient, right down to the smallest one, makes towards the dog's needs. This way you can be assured that each food has absolutely everything in the right amounts for your dog at each of the important life-stages every time you feed **Gilpa dog food.**

Gilbertson & Page Ltd. understand that every dog owner wants to do and obtain the best for their dog. The Premium Nutrition promise pledges that these factors are paramount in the design concept of each and every product in the **Gilpa range.**

Nutrition is about balance. An excess of any one nutrient or ingredient can be as disastrous as a deficiency. Equally an understanding of how nutrients and ingredients interact must be included in the recipe design of a great dog food. At **Gilbertson & Page Ltd.,** the nutrition and design team work to benefit every dog through the employment of nutritional knowledge from committed research, veterinary surgeons, animal behaviourists, and dedication to pets and pet owners. Sight is never lost of the fact that the food must be tasty and delicious to the dog not just the first time, but every day and thus great emphasis is placed on getting that extra special flavour that your dog will love.

Continuously striving for improvement means that the fixed recipes are always under review and, when appropriate, new additions to the life stage range of **Gilpa Pet Foods** are made to enhance the nutritional beneficial aspects of the diets without in any way upsetting the delicious taste.

Sometimes the quest for improved nutritional standards come as a first, for example Green lipped mussel extract in **Gilpa Kennel;** CLA in **Gilpa Slimline;** at other times they are a result of exploring and developing an existing concept such that the benefit to the dog is provided but without associated high costs. This maintains and enforces the promise of Premium Nutrition at a Sensible Price.

Good nutrition is about achieving a confidence. You will find it easy to be confident and comfortable with your choice of product from **Gilpa.**

Dog Training Instructor's Manual

First published 2000 by
Rainbow, PO Box 1044, Haxey, Doncaster. DN9 2JL.

Printed in the UK

ISBN 1-899057-02-1

Illustrations by Sarah Bales and Emma Lyons

Photographs by Mike White

Design, Layout and Printing by
New World Images Design & Print - 01302 719998

Acknowledgements

As we go to press, I celebrate 21 years of teaching dog training and animal behaviour. There are many people who have encouraged me to teach over the years, not least my husband and family - thank you all. Thanks must also go to my colleagues from Bishop Burton College, where I have been a lecturer in animal behaviour and training since 1992. The 'animal care team' have been most supportive.

I have been especially encouraged by all those who have attended my classes and courses, all over the world because, without their enthusiasm and support, I would not have been driven, or even wanted to carry on. Special thanks must go to all those who have seen fit to invite me to teach at their own venues, this has always been a real pleasure.

In the last few years I have taught many instructors, and for me, this has been the greatest buzz, to know that instructors are leaving me filled with enthusiasm to go on to teach others natural, motivational, humane and fun ways of training. So, to all those instructors, a heart felt thank you for helping me to spread the word.

Thanks also to my students of dog training who gave up their time to pose for photographs and to Sarah and Emma for the illustrations, good luck to you all for the future.

Thanks must also go to Tom Newbould for casting his expert literary eye over the text in the final edit.

And finally, thanks to all who take the time and effort to read this book, because I know you too will be out there spreading the word.

Chapter Index

About the Author

Angela White was born in the county of Yorkshire, England. She now resides in a remote village hamlet on the border of Yorkshire and Lincolnshire in the company of her husband Mike, son Daniel, and an assortment of dogs, (Leonbergers, Border collies, Pyrenean sheepdogs and an ageing Jack Russell), cats, two pet rats, a guinea pig, a goat, some sheep and two elderly chickens. Surrounded by woodland and country-side, she finds this an ideal retreat to indulge her passion of writing, when time allows, as well as being a base from which to run occasional courses on dog training and behaviour from a basic level through to teaching instructors and counsellors.

She is a part time consultant and lecturer in Animal Behaviour and Training at Bishop Burton College, where she enjoys passing on her knowledge to a wide variety of students. She sees this as a way of educating young minds before too many bad habits have time to get hold. She has been actively involved in creating a pathway into higher education in Animal Care and, specialising in training and behaviour, she has been able to help this progressive department of the college to provide a much needed avenue for those interested in working in this field.

As this, her fifth work on dog related subjects comes to fruition, she celebrates 21 years as an instructor of dog training. Over those 21 years she has studied, developed, and progressed her skills in both a scien-tific and practical way. Her main aim being to improve the lives of dogs, and those who choose to live and work with them, by increasing under-standing and finding easy ways to get the message across to humans and canines alike. Over those 21 years she has successfully operated her own training school and behavioural consultancy, as well as having been guest instructor and speaker for clubs, schools and societies around the UK and abroad.

In 1997 her book on competitive obedience, 'Happy Dogs Happy Winners' was translated into German and with this, came her close involvement in helping German dog trainers discover new and kind techniques of training. This culminated in the first obedience competi-tion in Germany being held in 1998, which would take the enthusiastic German obedience trainers into an entirely new area and encourage handlers to work towards the World championships organised by the F.C.I.. Angela is regularly invited to teach handlers and instructors in Germany and has a massive following all wanting to teach using natural behaviour with kindness, motivation and fun - the philosophy behind all of Angela's work.

As well as the UK and Germany Angela has travelled to many places around the world, teaching handlers and instructors how to enjoy their dogs, maintain control and be responsible dog owners. She teaches a huge diversity of levels ranging from dealing with behavioural problems, through to standard pet control, to Championship level obedience both to UK Kennel Club and F.C.I. regulations. Different countries have their own variation on competition rules but, Angela adjusts techniques to suit their needs, while still maintaining the all important concepts that makes her so unique and happily mirrored by disciples all over the world.

Angela enjoys teaching a wide variety of disciplines and over the years has either trained her own dogs or helped others on just about every dog sport imaginable. She is also an expert on cat behaviour and her knowledge of general behaviour has been sort to deal with horses and a variety of other pets too.

Angela with her Leonberger - Scout

Introduction

This work is based on the author's experience which has been gained, researched and accumulated over many years of teaching dogs, humans and other animals.

The dog training instructor has many responsibilities to the people that he or she teaches. The aim of this book is to help would-be instructors to take the right path in becoming successful and confident ambassadors of dog training.

The book is aimed at anyone wanting to teach others, but does assume that you already have some knowledge of dog training. If you are just starting as an instructor, the book gives constructive advice on how to get started both from a business point of view and a more general position. The more experienced instructor will gain from brushing up on up-to-date and new techniques and ideas, and will be able to develop their own dog school business or club with the aid of the advice and tips included.

It is a fact that the average dog owner will have preconceived ideas about what might be involved in dog training classes, or even at a one-to-one session, furthermore, few will realise the extent to which their own involvement will be relied upon to gain the desired results in their dog.

The dog owner will see the instructor demonstrate with their own dogs, handling difficult cases with ease, all of which gives a some what rose-tinted view. Of course all experienced handlers or instructors can make handling a dog look easy - the skill of the instructor is to teach the dog owners that it is not the instructor's magic powers, but techniques, timing and overall understanding that gets those impressive results.

It is a pointless exercise for an instructor to take a handler's dog to show them how good the dog can be, if the instructor cannot teach the handler how to achieve those results themselves.

Therefore, instructors must learn to teach in a way that the wide variety of pupils can understand, just as when he or she was a handler, the instructor learnt to teach their own dog in a way that he could understand.

A step by step approach, making sure that all the steps are included in a logical and practical order, coupled with a pleasant and caring attitude, will serve to educate pupils both canine and human, but of course all are different, so this also must be allowed for.

For instructors just starting out, the fact that knowledge and experience should be developed and built upon cannot be over emphasised - there is always something else we can learn.

The real dog enthusiast and good instructor will take their own dog training to an ever higher and diverse level and this will help the instructor to gain valuable experience. Handling a variety of breeds gives the hands on experience that cannot be learnt from books alone. Every opportunity should taken to build on experience - even if this means helping out at rescues or working in some other voluntary role.

Study canine behaviour - the instructor cannot rely solely on dog training techniques and exercises. An insight into human behaviour will also help instructors achieve their aims.

Instructors should not be afraid to look at other animals and their behaviour - this helps create a much fuller picture and actually helps things fit into place.

Overall the instructor's quest for knowledge will be virtually never ending - the instructor who thinks he knows it all has a lot to learn!

Setting up a Training School

Where To Teach

Permission To Run Your Business

The first thing to consider is where you are going to run your class. Some people are fortunate in that they have their own premises where dogs and public are already allowed. These are often establishments such as boarding kennels. If this is not the case, official permission to have dogs on a premises can be a problem, depending on the facility and the proximity to others.

You may not see your enterprise as a 'business' in the strictest sense of the word, but if you are going to charge for your teaching then that is what it is - no matter how low key. Even if it is to run as a club or society, (whether it is profit making or not), the same rules will apply as far as facilities are concerned. However, by putting forward a case which

Many trainers in the UK rent a hall for their training sessions

17

This is the instructors (and a few pupils who acted as stooges) at an instructors course for Hundefreunde Dachau, Germany, pictured in front of their excellent club house.

explains how you will give a service to the community, by helping to educate dog owners as to their control and responsibilities, may well give you a good defence if you have to give your reasons for setting up.

A house out in the country, with adjoining land and an agricultural building suitable for indoor teaching seems like the ideal solution, but even though the facility may seem ideal, it does not necessarily mean permission will be granted by the local authority, for regular training sessions. It will depend on suitability of access, numbers of cars/people expected and who else it will affect etc.

Setting up without permission can be costly and very disappointing, especially if you receive objections from owners and residents of neighbouring properties, it would be wise to follow the formal and correct channels to be on the safe side, before you invest time and money on facilities and advertising etc.

Type of Facility

On the continent is very common for dog clubs to have a club hut for the people to socialise, eat, drink, and hold meetings and talks. This is usually set in, or adjacent to, a field which is used for training, therefore all training is done outside. In the UK it is more the accepted norm to have an indoor facility, preferably with an outdoor area too although this is not essential for standard pet dog training.

Obviously if the weather is inclement, the ordinary members of the public are loathed to go out to do dog training and this is where an indoor facility comes into its own. If you intend to make the training school professional, then indoor training is a must. In the perfect world, a car park, a reasonable sized hall, a kitchen, toilets, a field and an office for consultations would be the best facilities and would cover all eventualities.

For many instructors, a hired hall and/or field will be the norm, and here, in order to keep your premises, you must be ultra careful in leaving the site free from hairs, faeces, urine and smells. Otherwise, irrespective of the fact that you are doing the community a service by teaching people how to be responsible dog owners, you could find yourself evicted. A typical case is where the hall or gardens are used as children's nurseries - any sign of hair on children's clothing and parents will be complaining. If the children's presence brings in more revenue than the dog club then no prizes for guessing who will be out first.

Who To Teach

An important issue is to assess the clientele and decide what is needed in your area. How many other training schools are there, and is there enough room for you too? Having said that, if you are good, you can start up the same type of training school as the one next door and you will soon get clientele.

If you are in a highly populated or an affluent area, puppy classes can be set up separately from the standard class. It is very beneficial to both dog and owner if puppies can be given a good start for a few weeks, before joining a class with adult dogs. In some areas it is not easy to get enough young puppies together at the same time to make a puppy class viable, but if this is the case, it is important that puppies and their owners are given attention, specific to their needs, and are positioned carefully in class so as to protect the pups from being bullied, frightened, or overpowered by larger or more boisterous dogs.

It is likely that as a dog trainer you have developed expertise in a specific area, agility, obedience, trials etc. You should be able to attract pupils in this field, obviously your facilities will need to be suitable for this teaching, but it is always a good idea to have a string to your bow that makes you unique. If you understand your sport fully, you should be able to teach and/or support at all levels. However, if you are unsure, start with the teaching of beginners and perhaps invite other levels to come for a work out and to use the facilities until you feel more confident. People will travel if you give a good and fair service, but don't try to be something that you are not.

Marketing Your Classes

Who Is Welcome

It is important to make it obvious who is welcome at your class when advertising. For instance, you could advertise '*Problem dogs welcome*', however, this does not mean you will get more than your fair share of problem dogs. Most owners think they have problems, but many of these 'problems' turn out to be normal behaviours that can be controlled with basic obedience exercises, with the addition of a few rules for sensible living. Occasionally you will encounter a behaviour case that is a real problem. These need to be dealt with separately, either by yourself if you feel suitably competent, or by a more experienced behavioural trainer or professional behavioural consultant. It may be appropriate to recommend the dog is seen by a veterinary surgeon to rule out any possible medical cause for the behaviour, certainly this is the best route if there is any reason for doubt.

Be specific about who and what you are teaching. For example, there is often confusion between obedience for pets and obedience for competitions. A pet owner will find it very unsatisfactory if they attend and find the obedience is not designed for pet control but more for competitive handlers and is beyond their reach.

Advertising - Find out where the local people get their information, for example is there a local newspaper that is popular? In some areas a free local newspaper is distributed to all except country locations. This is usually a good source for advertising. Also it is to your advantage to have cards and posters up in as many places as possible covering your catchment area. It is usually very inexpensive to advertise in newsagents and other shops. Your local vets may oblige too - have a word with the vet nurses - they are often the people who are asked for information on training classes because clients don't want to bother the vet with such trivialities. Many vet practices indeed welcome having somewhere to point new puppy owners. It is possible that the vet may be interested in you running small puppy parties at the surgery, its worth making an appointment to see the vet in charge to discuss this concept and its values for all concerned.

If you are a club rather than a business, the Library and/or local information service will also keep your information on file for anyone who cares to enquire.

More specialist training, competition work for example, should be advertised in the appropriate journals for the best results.

By far the best form of advertising is word of mouth, once you are up and running giving a good, honest and caring service, your problem is more likely to be one of waiting lists.

Selling The Course

Your initial contact with the client is of paramount importance, what you say and do then will determine whether you get the business. The client, having made the effort to get in touch, (normally by phone but possibly in person), is interested, but they need to be sold the value of the course, i.e. what benefits will they gain from coming along - so tell them! They will want to know what they can learn, and they will want to be assured that their problems will be addressed - well actually they will want to know whether their problems will be cured! You can't of course guarantee a cure because so much is down to what they do with the help that you give, but by asking questions you can assure them that the information will be available.

Incentive to Attend - Ask if they have any problems, but ask in a specific way, for instance, 'Does he pull?' Most will answer 'yes', and then you can assure them that this will be covered and they will be taught how to enjoy taking the dog for a walk instead of being pulled down the road. If they say no, say how lucky they are and suggest another common problem, they may at this point tell you the problem that is bugging them. Of course there is very little you can't cover.

Discussing Cost - The cost is the only negative part of the conversation, but when compared to something like driving lessons it is bound to be attractive, and the benefits far outweigh the cost, particularly if you explain the value of such a course versus the cost of private consultation if they leave the problems to get worse.

Of course cost is not just about money. For many busy people time and effort is just as important, so this must be included in the equation. The client will no doubt determine the value of the course in his/her own terms, but it is a good idea to have some form of bonus that the client is not expecting. For instance you could issue certificates on completion of the course and you could throw in a free gift - many feed companies love to sponsor with free samples of their dog food. Another good incentive is to include a 'free' dog lead with the cost of the course. Even the added bonus of advice on nutrition, grooming, general care etc. will help sell your services. Added bonuses that are not expected or assumed add value to the course and will make the client choose you over others - as

long as your quality is at least comparable.

Be Their Friend - Your phone manner is also important if you want to secure this and future business, you should respond in a warm and friendly manner, and make the client feel valued. Some clients may seem awkward or demanding, but if you keep your cool, follow the rules of good relationships and convert the client you will be in business for life, because a satisfied customer guarantees lots of enthusiastic recommendations.

Insurance - Insurance is a must. You at least need public liability cover, if you employ others you will need employees liability. Speak to your insurance broker or advisor to find out what will be best for you. Also, look in the canine press, there are some companies who specialise in this type of insurance, and you may get a better deal, plus a purpose built scheme that covers all eventualities.

Forward Planning

As discussed previously, the first contact you will have with your potential client is likely to be on the phone, when they ring to enquire about coming to class. At this stage most clients will already own a dog, in some cases it may be 6 months old or more. They have called because they feel its time to start training or because problems are starting to occur. It is necessary to get as much information as you can from the person regarding their dog and their circumstances in order to slot them into the correct and most suitable class, and to ascertain whether they need additional specialised or private help. Of course the age and breed of the dog and the way the owner portrays the animal will give you a good idea, but you may have to ask more questions to work out whether what the owner considers to be a problem can be addressed in class or not.

It is of paramount importance not to put other dogs or their owners at risk from dogs that may have become aggressive, or are so out of control that the owners cannot cope, indeed it would be unfair to put the owner of a problem dog in a situation where they could not feel confident and in control. Therefore, these more severe problems must be identified and addressed outside the class environment initially. Once the problem is under the owner's control, the dog can, and often should be, integrated into class to enable the owner to continue working on the problem. This will also help you to keep in contact giving assistance and encouragement along the way. Occasionally a problem behaviour is aggravated by a class situation and therefore you will need to exercise your professional discretion on this.(See *Problem Behaviours and Growl classes*).

Time for Questions - There are many questions that the new puppy or dog owner will want to ask about the training class. Some ask, others don't, but all should be given the opportunity to find out what they need to know.

It is of great benefit to both instructor and client to have, following the initial phone call and discussion on attending class, an information sheet, sent by post, covering all the common questions. (Turn to *appendix* 2 and you will see the sort of thing that you could consider sending. Of course deck it out with your own club/school logos, details and specialisms).

It is also a good idea, and portrays a very professional style, to enrol the pupils by getting them to fill in a booking form (See *appendix* 2). Depending on how far in advance you are working, this completed form can be brought along by the client on the first night of class, or better still sent back in the post with payment to secure their place in class. Advance booking avoids the hazards of over booking. When sent back to you in advance, the information on the form enables you organise your enrolment night. You will know who is coming, where to position people, what breeds and potential problems you may have and so on.

What To Teach

Pet Training

There are certain things that must be taught, and as the instructor you will have to know a variety of ways to achieve these goals, in order to be successful with all the differing types of dogs and handler that you are confronted with. Of course most instructors have their favoured and most successful techniques and these are the ones that are used in the first instance. (*See training techniques for a good selection - add your own as you progress*). Sometimes you have to be adaptable and find a different way to achieve the desired result.

The basic exercises for pet control must include: Walking on a loose lead (walking to heel), come back when called (recall), sit, down, stand (for general control, veterinary inspection or to be groomed), leave on command, not to pull through openings (doors etc.), not to jump up.

Many other areas need to be addressed including the possible household problems that may be occurring, this can often be done in a question and answer session, but you may have to set the ball rolling with a discussion on a commonly asked question like how to stop chewing furniture and fittings etc. in the home.

Specialist Subjects

What to teach in other more specialised areas must depend on your own experience and strengths. For example, it is pointless setting up to teach competitive obedience if you are not accustomed to all of the idiosyncrasies involved in this highly competitive and very precise sport. To be competent means you need to have competed or been actively involved yourself, not too long ago, to a reasonable level, and to be aware of current trends. If you cannot meet this criteria you will not keep your students for very long. Of course any instructor worth his salt, can teach a dog to be obedient. However, the competition world is a whole different ball game.

Disciplines like agility and flyball can be taught for fun, as can the more advanced obedience exercises, and many dog owners enjoy their weekly round on the agility course, at the flyball box or taking part in the complexities of scent discrimination, distance control, sendaways etc.

If you are not already an expert, make sure that you are fully conversant with all the safety rules before you set out to teach any of the disciplines involving equipment, even if it is 'just for fun'. You would also find it of benefit to talk to an expert trainer in the proposed field before embarking on your teaching. You could check if any of the methods you have in mind would cause problems, should the client decide they want to take the sport further and become competitive.

As in all teaching of psychomotor skills, it is of paramount importance that the instructor can actually achieve the exercise that he/she is teaching. In other words don't start teaching pupils to do something before you have achieved the skill yourself on a number of occasions with a variety of dogs, and feel competent that you can step in and take over if the need should arise.

Work with your strengths, only set out to teach what you know you excel in. It is rather like writing a book, the experts always advise to write from experience, as that experience grows so too can your teaching.

Basic Resources

What You Will Need

Basic requirements such as pen, writing pad, cash till and float are a necessary part of any business where clients are to be dealt with face to face. But there are many other resources that should be taken into consideration to make things run more smoothly, promote a professional atmosphere and give your clients good value for money, whilst maintaining a safe and comfortable environment for all.

Toys and Titbits - While you may ask owners to bring along toys and titbits to motivate their dogs, it is best to provide a variety of suitable items yourself too, (a) because some will forget, and (b) because some will bring things that are not attractive to or suitable for their dogs. The dog may well love that toy at home but, if it has free access to it, the toy will loose its appeal when there are other dogs around creating a greater distraction.

Very palatable titbits will also be beneficial, again at home the dog may love bits of biscuit, but it sometimes takes something a little more special to get the pup's attention in class. By providing a selection you will also be able to demonstrate the benefits of the more suitable toys and titbits. Have some available for handlers to use, but also have some on sale to help your profits

Leads, Collars, etc. - It will be of benefit to have available for loan or for sale, suitable collars and leads. Crates or indoor kennels will be a good idea to show the owners and to explain the benefits, many of them will never have seen one. Some dog schools sell crates or loan them out in a variety of sizes. Rather an expensive investment but well worth it.

Cleaning Materials - Don't forget a supply of poo bags, some handlers may never have seen let alone used one! To promote responsible hygiene set a good example with your own dogs at all times. Other cleaning equipment will be needed to clean up accidents and get rid of hair and other rubbish in the training hall or ground e.g. mop and bucket, shovel, sawdust, disinfectant, refuse bags and sweeping brush.

Drinking Water - It is not a good idea to supply communal water, although many dog schools do - rather encourage owners to bring their own, a communal drinking bowl is an ideal place for breeding germs and encouraging cross infections.

Indoor Training Facilities

Handlers of small dogs or puppies will spend time on the floor

Floor Surface - Ideally you need to create an environment where at times, owners will feel comfortable sitting or kneeling on the floor with their dog. Although this is not essential, and indeed some owners will not be able to manage because of physical problems, but it does help at times to get down to dog level, especially in puppy classes. Therefore, ensure that the floor is clean and free from dog hairs before class starts, and if possible, provide some washable matting for owners to sit or kneel on. The floor should be disinfected on a reasonably regular basis and always after accidents or before puppy classes.

Slippery floor surfaces can be hazardous, and therefore if you are using a hall with this type of floor you will need to invest in some rubber matting to stop the dogs slipping.

Make sure the floor is free from debris and defects that may cause accident or injury. I do know of one dog club who were sued by a pupil who slipped on a wet surface (caused by condensation) and broke her arm.

Temperature - The exact temperature is not crucial, but try to aim for a comfortable temperature on the cool rather than hot side. It is important to create a good air flow, particularly in the summer, to help prevent the spread and harbouring of airborne disease such as kennel cough. In winter it is good to take the chill off, but owners can and should be advised to dress appropriately, once they start working with the dog they will warm up.

Seating - Though not essential seating is a good idea if at all possible. There will always be times when you require your pupils to stop and listen or to watch others. Seating also seems to break the ice and make people feel more comfortable. It also encourages partners and other family members to come along. This is good because then all of the family can be learning the right way to handle the dog instead of just one. I have taught without seating but I find that it is less convenient for the theory side of training, and because people are standing around, you find yourself wanting to keep them moving more than perhaps is practical.

Ideally the seating should allow pupils to have sufficient room between themselves and the next person to create a comfortable distance in which to control their dog. It may be necessary to seat your pupils in specific areas to prevent inter-reaction between dogs. If not you may create problems that new dog owners will struggle to control at the outset.

Lighting - This might seem obvious but recently I was asked to teach in an indoor area where the lighting was so poor I could not see the expressions on the pupils faces. The facility must be well lit, especially for evening teaching.

Outdoors Facilities

Teaching outside has benefits and draw backs. It means that the class can spread out, but this makes it more difficult to hold the group together. I don't mind teaching more advanced groups in this way but find beginners need a physical structure so, if outside, I put up a ring to save them from straying too far.

If you are teaching on grass this can be a simple structure of show ring posts or sheep fencing posts and light rope. If you are on a solid surface you will need to get some free-standing posts or perhaps simply set out some bollards to work within.

If the class is large or is to be allowed to spread out I 'condition' the owners to respond to my whistle (a simple gundog type), they are asked to stop what they are doing when they hear it and come back to listen

Ring ropes can help to keep your class within your reach

to what I have to say.

Of course there is also the issue of safety from outside influences. You need to consider the relative importance of fencing to control outsiders including people, dogs, livestock or even traffic.

The weather can be your enemy outside as can the light if teaching in the evenings. Some schools do manage with outdoor facilities only, but you need to be prepared for a very low turn out in bad weather. If you teach a course where clients pay in advance they may not be happy if poor weather inhibits their ability to learn and get full value for their money.

The surface outside is important too, long grass can be wet, slippery and may lead to pupils tripping. Small dogs can not be expected to do accurate work in long grass, and may well grow tired quickly from constantly having to hop over large clumps. Uneven ground can also be dangerous as can wet or muddy conditions. Certainly specific advice on footwear must be given depending of the type of surface you are working on, but definitely no high heels!

The ideal, of course, is a facility with both indoor and outdoor facilities so you can make your choice depending on the weather and the type of group that you are teaching.

Other Facilities

Car Parking - You may not think this is your problem if you hire a hall, but when local residents complain about dogs, cars and noise suddenly it becomes your problem. Therefore take this into consideration when organising your classes. Equally if you have your own premises, car parking can make a difference. Many people do not like to attend an event that has difficult parking and will be easily put off, especially when attending in the dark. So try to arrange a clear, well lit, easily accessible car park, suitable for the amount of pupils expected. Perhaps the car park size needs to be taken into account when deciding on class/group sizes.

Catering - Some classes see this as a crucial part of their set up. Certainly cups of tea, coffee or soft drinks will help to keep the classes on a social level, and encourage pupils to stop and chat. Single handed instructors cannot really attempt catering without help. Don't let your quality of instruction lapse for the sake of making a pot of tea! Its your expertise in dog training and behaviour that they are paying for.

Emergency Procedures - Make sure that all fire and emergency exits including assembly areas are clearly marked, and point them out to pupils on their first night. Make sure that all emergency exits are in good working order and not blocked at any time. Make sure your premises has been checked by a fire officer and that fire extinguishers are regularly maintained and available for use at all times.

A fully stocked first aid kit should be available for both owners and dogs. Consult with your veterinary surgeon regarding the latter.

FIRE EXIT
KEEP CLEAR

S Bones

Your local vet should be aware of your teaching timetable, and his phone number should be displayed in a prominent position. Remember, if you are not a qualified veterinary surgeon yourself, it is not a good idea to treat someone else's pet. In the UK it is illegal so leave it to the experts.

In the event of an emergency make sure you follow all the appropriate guidelines and maintain a calm and controlled attitude.

Background Information

Information Required By All Owners

You will find that dog owners, especially those very new to the concept of owning, caring for and controlling a dog, need much more information than is perhaps apparent.

When they first come to dog training classes they will of course expect to learn about dog training, but there are many other areas that can, and need to be covered, whether teaching owners of puppies or older dogs. Giving good all round information will help owners achieve their aims, because as you know, dogs like humans, need to feel good in order to lead a happy and well adjusted life. Without proper care, dogs will not have that 'feel good' factor and therefore will not be so receptive to learning.

Nutrition - All responsible breeders give diet sheets to new dog owners, but it is not unusual for owners to either disregard, or miss-understand the information given. Some diets are complicated, others far too vague, and often new and experienced owners alike are confused over how to progress, how much food to give and when to stop feeding extra meals and so on.

The Veterinary Surgeon is often the first professional that the new puppy owner will consult, and diet changes are frequently recommended for a variety of reasons, particularly if the pup has digestive disorders, weight fluctuations or other possible food related problems. It is not unusual, therefore, for the owner to become even more confused. Pet owners are often overawed (although not intentionally) by their veterinary surgeon, and they forget to ask questions, or perhaps do not think of those questions at the time of the appointment, then they puzzle over their queries later, perhaps seeking advice from friends or family - this advice, though well intended, is not always accurate or appropriate.

As the instructor, you can perhaps be more easily approached on a friendly level, giving more time and help to those who require it. It is

33

worth learning as much as you can on the subject of nutrition, but you don't need to be an expert to know that all dogs must have a balanced diet suitable for their age, size and activity. Common 'dog sense' can prevail from here and will make owners (and therefore their dogs) feel much better.

Here is some general advice that I have found useful over the years;

1 Feed your dog to **condition** rather than worrying about amounts quoted on packets or tins. For instance the dog should be neither under nor over weight, have adequate but not excessive energy for its breed, and be in good condition generally.

2 If owners are feeding a tinned food, they should feed the mixer that is recommended to go with that particular tinned food, to be sure of the correct balance.

3 Dry foods can of course be fed dry, but are easier to digest if soaked with warm water, and it is my belief that making sure that the dog has a good intake of water by adding it to the diet, you will help to guard against many of the major diseases and problems brought about by dehydration. Dogs and humans for that matter need far more water than most people think and internal dehydration can be a problem long before any of the more obvious signs are seen.

4 Deep chested dogs should be fed at head level, i.e. off the ground to help avoid gastric torsion. Current research suggests that dogs fed a variety of foods rather than sticking to just one food are less likely to suffer torsion.

5 Don't give exercise immediately before or after feeding. Ideally at least an hour should be allowed either side for the animal to rest and start to digest its food. Obviously pups need to eliminate (go to the toilet) after feeding, but they should be taken to an appropriate area, restricted to prevent too much running around, allowed to 'go', and then taken to a quiet area to rest.

6 Avoid giving too many extra treats. When treats are used in training, make sure they are taken into consideration as part of the dog's normal diet, therefore titbits should be nutritious and balanced against other intake. Ideally use part of the animal's dinner. Avoid sweet sugary treats.

7 Not all foods suit all breeds, types or pockets. Try to avoid being 'brand blind', have an open mind and advise, based on experience of the breed. Remember to take into consideration all other factors, including breeder/vet recommendations, activity level, age, health, condition etc.

Exercise - Exercise is often a neglected subject, and many owners live with the misguided opinion that, the larger the dog, the more exercise it needs. Of course too much exercise, especially for growing limbs, can be as bad if not worse than not enough exercise.

Puppies need free play to develop their bodies, but should not be pushed on long treks or even in play sessions longer than is good for them. Even 10 minutes walk at a brisk pace can be too much for a very young puppy of a large or heavy breed like a Leonberger or New-foundland. Large breeds mature, mentally and physically, at a much slower rate than smaller breeds, therefore it will be quite a while before they can go out on a long walk. Realistically you are looking at 18 months old, (sometimes a little older if they are really heavy boned), before they reach their full potential, and

Owners of large boned puppies need special guidelines regarding exercise.

then there must be a very gradual build up to strengthen muscle and stamina.

Of course, at 5 or 6 months old the pup that gets little or no exercise will be a hooligan to live with. Owners should be taught how to give their pets lots of stimulating exercise and play, learning new things and enjoying different environments, but keeping actual walking and running to the amount that would be a naturally occurring level. This can mean taking the dog out in the car, or on the bus to get to interesting places, much as you would if you were bringing up a toddler. If the dog is confined to the garden until he is 18 months old, the animal will drive the owners, and itself mad, and of course his social skills will be badly affected by neglect.

Slippery floors, and steep steps can also cause problems for growing limbs, and again, even if informed by the breeder, it is easy for new puppy owners to forget, or perhaps not appreciate the importance of protecting their pet in this way. Ramps and/or matting may need to be put in place to protect the pup during the growth stages.

Worming and Inoculation - Hopefully all dogs will have been inoculated and wormed before you, as the instructor, see them. Having said that, new owners may well require additional information on how to progress; what to do if they are going to put their pet in boarding kennels; when to give the next worming tablets; some owners may not even be aware that they should continue to treat their animal after the initial puppy medications.

Grooming, bathing, nail trimming - This of course depends on breed and environment, but all dogs should be groomed as part of the social interaction between dog and owner.

It is a good idea to include sessions on grooming in class, and give special attention to those less likely to groom their dogs on a very regular basis, i.e. those with short coated breeds such as Rottweillers, Dobermanns, Bull Terriers, Boxers, Jack Russells etc., all powerful characters who could become dominant. Controlled social grooming sessions will help to assert owner control. Owners should also be able to touch all parts of the dog's body, and even if nails do not require clipping, owners should be shown how to gain the dog's confidence and achieve this without a struggle. This can be justified by explaining how a veterinary surgeon will need to examine the dog should it fall ill or be

injured in any way, therefore it is a useful exercise to get the owners to teach the dog to be examined.

Dogs and the Law - The law relating to dogs and other animals varies depending on: (a) the country and (b) the local bylaws. As an instructor you will be promoting responsible dog ownership as a concept, therefore you must be aware of the law and be able to give advice on how this affects all dog owners in your vicinity. For example, in the UK, at the time of writing, the Dangerous Dogs Act names some breeds for special conditions, but it is meant to apply to all breeds - many dog owners are totally unaware of this.

Identification of dogs is also an important issue that owners may not understand fully. In the UK (at the time of writing), dogs must wear an identification tag that clearly states the owner's name and address - in some countries dogs must have more permanent registered identification such as a tattoo or microchip. Regulations regarding taking the dog outside of their own country also vary. Instructors should know and be able to give advice on local authority as well as the country's laws, rules and regulations.

One of the favourite goals for many dog owners is to walk their dog off lead. They may not be aware that, even when they achieve this level of control, it will be an offence to do so on certain roads and in certain areas.

Hygiene - All dog owners should be instructed and expected to clean up after their dogs in all situations. Implements to do this, poo bags, shovels etc., should be available in class. Owners should be made aware of the necessity to pick up their dog's mess wherever they are - not just at class.

Owners should also be given advice on how to prevent and treat infestations of fleas, ticks, worms and other common internal and external parasites, both on the animal and in the home or kennel environment.

From time to time certain diseases could become a specific problem in your area - it is a good idea to understand the basic infection routes and signs of illness such as parvovirus, distemper, kennel cough, leptospirosis and rabies etc. It may seem a little simplistic, but advice on hand washing and very basic hygiene may also be appropriate.

Poisons, Toxins and Other Hazards - Many owners are not aware of potential dangers to dogs, in the home, the garden, and in the countryside. Of course it is simple to suggest that 'toddler' rules are followed regarding household chemicals, i.e. keep them locked away, but it should be remembered that the young pup may be more agile than a 2 year old child, and what may be out of reach for a toddler may be a 'piece of cake', if you'll pardon the pun, for the lively pup.

Garden Hazards - Most children don't tend to chew garden plants, but puppies do - so owners need to be aware of potentially poisonous plants some of the more common ones include: Rhododendron, Rhubarb leaves, Laburnum, Yew, Wisteria seeds, English Ivy, Fox Gloves, many bulbs and tubers. Of course there are many more, and owners should really be educating their pets to not chew any garden plants by providing them with a supply of varying and interesting chew toys and keeping them well away from hazardous areas or plants.

Chocolate - It is amazing how many people are not aware that chocolate is potentially dangerous to dogs, unless it is made specifically for them. The human variety contains theobromine, a 100 gm bar of chocolate contains 160 mg of theobromine which is enough to kill a small dog.

Toys - Even some toys that are designed for dogs can be toxic if ingested. Only toys specifically designed as chew toys, and suitable for the breed and age of the dog, are safe to leave with the dog while he is unsupervised.

Household Dangers and Garden Dangers - There are many other dangers in the household, loose or exposed electrical wires, small objects like needles, decorations (especially at Christmas time), rubbish bins containing sharp tins, glass, cooked bones (especially chicken bones) and so on.

Dogs can become very resourceful and if left unattended, they can work out how to open cupboards and even refrigerators - child locks normally deal with these sort of problems - but advice should be given on why the dog is resorting to these and other undesirable behaviours that may be potentially dangerous. Owners need to be educated in how to stimulate the dog so that he is ready to sleep, play with or chew appropriate items when left for short periods. (*See Problem Behaviours - Separation Problems*).

Garden ponds can also be hazardous - the best advice is to block the pup's access to such areas until he is old enough to understand not to go near it or to cope should he go in.

It goes without saying (hopefully) that the garden should be fenced and puppy proof. Fencing that keeps fully grown dogs contained may not be adequate for a small pup. Very tiny pups can get their mouths caught on wire mesh so should not be left unattended or out of earshot. If they do get caught they will soon yell and let the owner know.

As mentioned before (*see exercise*) slippery floors, steps, stairs, etc. can be dangerous for growing limbs, therefore precautions must be taken.

House Training - Of course many pups will be clean in the house, barring the odd accident, by the time they come to class, but some owners may still be experiencing problems and be too embarrassed to ask, so make sure you cover this and also be flexible in the way you approach the problem, taking into account differing domestic arrangements.

Behavioural Information - It is necessary to cover all basic problems that may occur: biting, chewing, barking, chasing, growling, dominance and separation problems etc. These are not problems that are likely to occur in class, but they should never the less be covered because, you can guarantee that everyone in the class will be experiencing one, if not more, of these behavioural problems and they are easily dealt with by an instructor who has insight.

Training Exercises - There are five basic exercises that will give the owner control of the dog once they have mastered them. These are to get the dog to; sit, lay down, come when called, walk to heel without pulling, and leave on command. Of course there are many other things that can be taught, but in puppy or beginner class these are the basics that will give them a good start and help to control other potential problems, for example if a dog is sitting he cannot be jumping up.

Social Training - Apart from the general training exercises there are some very important aspects which must be concentrated on in class, because these may mean the difference between life and death to the dog. For instance the dog must know how to react when grabbed from behind, nipped or tugged by a child, what to do when visitors come to the home, what to do when approached by a stranger, how to inhibit its bite when playing with humans. If the dog behaves aggressively or even just incorrectly, this could mean the owners reach a point where they feel their lives would be better without him and therefore, make the decision to part with the dog. Sadly, statistics tell us that the vast majority of dogs that leave their first home end up being destroyed. Even if they do find second homes, many dogs will end up back with the welfare organisations, purely because they haven't been taught the rules of living with humans when they were younger. As they mature, the problem becomes more difficult to deal with, no matter how determined the new owner is.

Canine Psychology - It is important to give the owner an insight into the psychology of canine learning and training, this can be brief, but they must understand that the dog does not think like we do. Many owners will expect great things from their dogs, especially as they start to grow and develop, and if the results are not forthcoming, they will blame the dog for being, naughty, stubborn etc., before they look to themselves for errors in training. It is a common fault in most humans, to lay the blame on others when things do not go according to plan, but a little understanding and encouragement to learn more, may help owners to look further than what they see in front of them.

Responsible Dog Ownership - Owners should be taught the importance of sound dog training, showing them headlines from a newspaper covering a dog attack may bring the message home. No matter how large or small, if their dog bites someone, for whatever reason, the chances are their dog will be euthanased, or not to put too finer point on it, 'killed'. There is also the more profound affect, i.e. whatever their dog does has an affect on dogs and their owners in general. Every time dogs are allowed to misbehave and, in so doing, make the headlines or upset someone, the likelihood for even more restricted access for dogs and their owners increases. Their problematic behaviour gives rise to changes in the laws and bylaws which are designed to protect the innocent.

Principles of Instructing

Before you can be a successful instructor you must gain sufficient knowledge to make you competent and comfortable with any problems posed to you. Of course we can't all be over-night Einstein's but, before teaching others you should at least have a sound basic knowledge that you are able to apply in a number of situations, to a variety of breeds, and know when and where to turn to seek more advanced or appropriate advice if need be.

What Makes a Good Instructor?

To be good instructor requires a good working knowledge of human psychology as well as canine understanding. This does not mean you need a degree, but it is well worth studying some basics to give you an insight into the human mind.

The instructor requires many qualities including patience, dedication, knowledge and understanding. You must be well focused yet flexible, have a friendly attitude, oodles of tact and diplomacy and a genuine love for dogs and their people.

Of course on top of all that you must have the ability to take control of a class, project your voice, understand about positioning so that all can hear and see, teach in a manner that holds the interest, know when to liven things up and when to calm things down. You need to be able to anticipate, recognise and guide dogs and owners away from problems. Have the appropriate knowledge and foresight to ask the right questions to help you to make accurate diagnoses of problems, and therefore give appropriate advice. Read canine and human body language, recognise the significance of eye contact, and assess dogs and their owners continuously.

If you set up a training school on your own, you must also have business skills to organise and run the classes efficiently and effectively, taking into consideration profitability, tax, insurance, and other allied responsibilities, as well as offering and delivering a good, professional and honest service.

So, as you can see, it is not just a case of being able to handle, train and control dogs - it is equally important to be able to handle people - the dog training part can be very easy in comparison! Just as the dog needs to learn that his owner is the most important person in the room, so you must learn to make the owner feel important too.

Their problems are very real, and although, when you as the instructor see the owner and their pet for an hour a week, the problem may seem trivial, always remember what it is like to live with that problem for 24 hours a day.

Patience is a great virtue and good listening skills a must, patience is needed with the animals, but just as important, patience, tact and diplomacy is needed with the owners.

The Owner's Concept of Dog Class

Many owners will expect their dog to be miraculously trained at the end of the training course, or sooner, and will rarely be prepared for the work involved. Some will expect you to train the dog for them, some will even expect the dog to watch and learn! Yes, we had 'that man', who sat at the side of the hall, with his chocolate Labrador, telling the dog to watch us, while we demonstrated with a dog, and then he got annoyed when his dog looked away, he said to him, "Watch or you will never learn", and yes, he was serious! Thank goodness this doesn't happen too often. On every course there are enough sensible people, who know that they are the ones who are there to learn and that part of the learning involves finding out how to be a team with their dog.

The people who attend dog classes are, on the whole, caring individuals who want the best for their dogs. There may be a few who are there through desperation, they may even feel that the dog class is the last resort, i.e. if you can't teach their dog a lesson it will have to go! But those who feel that way are thankfully few. Most people who have a strong negative feeling about their dog's behaviour, unfortunately for the dog, will not bother to attend classes. Therefore, one can assume that the caring owners who do attend want the best for their dogs.

Giving dog owners an understanding of why methods of training are chosen, and how and why they work, will help them to be successful and confident in what they are trying to achieve.

All owners will enjoy talking about their pet, and will want to feel that you, the instructor, see them as special. It is well worth spending a little time with each owner and dog. A good time is as they arrive, generally chatting, giving the dog a titbit or a stroke, and asking how they are getting on. This will boost confidence and give them a chance to talk, one to one, about any problems. This time will also give you a chance to assess them and their dog.

Praise the owners for any improvements, no matter how small. If you can find nothing to praise in their training find something nice to say about the dog. "Hasn't she grown". "Does that tail ever stop wagging?" "What a beautiful pup!" There has to be something that will make them feel special. Owners as well as dogs thrive in an atmosphere that is rewarding and pleasant. It is always good form to try to remember the dog's name, even if you can't remember the owners! They like to feel that you are on personal terms with their dog.

Knowing the Breeds

An understanding of a wide variety of breeds, including any local varieties, is essential.

Almost all breeds have their own set of idiosyncrasies, for example:

* Leonbergers and Newfoundlands love water, and therefore the owner will have to deal with a dog who shares his water with the kitchen floor, and with all whom he loves!
* The Border Collie is bred to work and run. Being confined to a domestic environment owners may have to contend with a dog that chases cycles, joggers, the cat, or in fact anything that moves, he may even try to herd the children!
* Terriers are bred to go to ground for vermin, so they will love to dig, they play rough games, and are often very noisy.

* Labradors love to have things in their mouths, and their brain is ruled by their stomach.
* Cocker Spaniels are said to carry aggressive tendencies - dominance and idiopathic, *(see problem behaviours)*, with this knowledge, it is easy to jump to conclusions (often unfounded) whenever you see a Cocker, especially solid colours.
* German Shepherd dogs are prone to fear related behaviours, sometimes coming out in aggression, they are highly reactive to their senses which can make them rather a handful for the uninitiated.
* Many of the toy breeds are bred as companion dogs and have strong attachment behaviours, often demanding to be picked up in times of stress. They are also very prone to learning to guard their space in the home.
* Huskies and the like are bred to pull, so walking to heel can be a challenge.
* Afghans and other hounds are bred to run, so when let off the lead that is what they do, making recalls very difficult!

* Greyhounds are bred to chase furry animals so careful integration with cats and other animals is needed.

There are also certain problems that breeders have created by altering the look of the dogs:

* Samoyeds, they have been bred to have a sticking up coat, tail carried high and pointed ears - all signs of a dominant dog, whether he likes it or not, the Samoyed gives off the wrong signals to other dogs.

✱ Boxers have wrinkled up flat faces and often no tail at all, again it is not easy for 'normal' dogs to read the canine body language from this breed, so extra care and attention must be given during socialisation. You must realise that dogs that have exaggerated or unusual features will not be so acceptable to other dogs, unless they have had good previous experiences with the breed in question.

The list of idiosyncrasies is endless. If you are just starting out as an instructor, or if you have limited experience with breeds other than your own, it is best to read up on what the various types were originally bred for, including the behaviour and health problems associated with those breeds, as you come into contact with them. This way you will build on your knowledge as you go along.

This is another good reason to apply an advance booking system to your classes, i.e. sending out questionnaires to secure places (*see appendix 2*), this will give you time to find out which breeds are going to attend and to read up on any that you are not accustomed to, before you have to deal with them in class.

Knowing Dogs

Of course a huge knowledge of dogs in general is essential, and this can only be gained with experience, study and time.

For instance: understanding how dogs react together, how they react if brought up with other dogs, the interaction and bonding between two puppies brought up together, dogs reared as the only canine, dogs living with children, dogs weaned or leaving the litter too early, dogs acquired over 12 weeks of age and so on.

As an instructor, it is necessary to know that it is perhaps not ideal to have two pups together because, unless they are treated as individuals, they will bond and tend to work as a team, making handling more difficult. Instructors should realise that it is always best to get a pup when it is around 7 - 8 weeks of age, because this is the ideal point in the early socialisation period for the dog to adapt. (*See canine development and learning*).

Knowledge like this and much more is an essential part of your professionalism. However, the owners will already have come to you with problems related to these areas. Telling them they have made a mistake in purchasing this dog it is not the answer they are looking for. Although explanations of the behaviours will help them understand, they will still need solutions.

Therefore, it is imperative that you study canine behaviour, and have a broad understanding of why problems occur, how to prevent them, but most essentially, how to deal with them. You will need to put into force programmes for correction of behaviour that will at least make life bearable for the owner.

Canine Body Language

Understanding the dog's body language can help to prevent problems and indeed enhance training techniques and procedures. The dog communicates more with his body than he does vocally and therefore we need to know what he is saying.

Of course we should be aware that there are variations on these basic postures. For example, dogs can be quite dominant in a fearful way, they can also be submissive and fearful or confidently submissive.

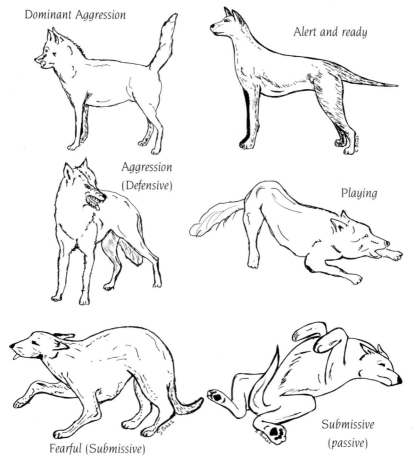

Dominant Aggression

Alert and ready

Aggression (Defensive)

Playing

Fearful (Submissive)

Submissive (passive)

As discussed above, in some breeds of dog the natural ear, tail, posture or coat can give misleading signals to you but, more especially to other dogs.

Using your own posture and head signals and educating the owners to do the same, you can influence the dog's behaviour. For example if you turn away and lower your posture on recalls the dog is more likely to come to you. If you lean forward towards the dog he is more likely to back off.

It is a good idea to study the posturing and subtle signals of communication amongst wolves. A turn of the head is a signal made when a wolf wants to turn off another wolf's anger or to communicate the fact that he is not a threat. They often use other signals too, for example sniffing, circling, looking away, yawning, licking their own nose - all signals that say 'please don't hurt me'. Sometimes the signals are very quick and the reaction from the other wolves subtle but, with practice you will read the signs. You can use the head turning in the same way that the dog does, try it on your own dogs. It is especially useful when dealing with dogs who have not had a good start in life, or who have been brought up more in the company of other dogs than of humans. Some breeds are especially sensitive to body language, typically those breeds who are known in more general terms to be sensitive for example; Border collies, German shepherd dogs and Pyrenean sheepdogs.

It' is normal behaviour for animals to split up if they feel they are getting too close, this avoids or calms conflict. Therefore, mimicking this, the instructor physically going between dogs who are becoming tense or aggressive towards each other, is often enough to prevent a situation getting out of hand. Also encouraging the owners to put themselves between the dogs will help. Obviously there are times when dogs are better placed well apart but, this should not be seen as a failure, one should accept that, like people, some dogs are never going to be buddies.

Setting A Good Example

Even dog training instructors are human, and occasionally your own programme of training will go wrong. However, the dog owner will note how you deal with your own animals, and should be able to learn appropriately from your example.

It is not your place to show off your handling abilities to the determent of others, although of course the occasional demonstration will go down well to show the skills needed and to prove that they work.

I was very proud when a student of mine brought a group of her own students to watch me in the obedience ring with a novice dog on his first time in test 'A' (the next class up). Of course the dog did not perform perfectly, and I could overhear my student saying to her students, "yes, its gone wrong, but watch what she does now". She could say this in full knowledge that, whatever I chose to do after my dog had gone to urinate on the fence instead of retrieving his dumbbell, she would not see me harsh handle the dog or loose my cool.

One example of very unprofessional use of knowledge I observed was an instructor repeatedly and deliberately inciting a client's dog into inter-male and protective aggression by the use of her own male dog, her own body language and eye contact. She did this just to show an observer how bad the other dog could be. The poor dog owner was left to try to deal with the rather large Dobermann on his own while the instructor gloated at his lack of control - the very reason that he had come in search of help.

Choice of Techniques

Sometimes owners will not agree with something that you suggest. All modern training should be based on sound behavioural knowledge, and no harsh or punitive techniques need be demonstrated. Therefore, if you are following this regime, you can be happy that there is nothing that will hurt the dog. If an owner does disagree, be tactful, hear them out, and then explain your case in another way. If they still do not agree, perhaps you can find a different way of doing things that they find more acceptable, perhaps you can ask what they had in mind and then you can either use or adapt their ideas, or if necessary explain why that method is not suitable. There is always more than one way of training or dealing with a problem, but stick to your principles and explain how what you suggest will work, is humane, and for the good of the dog and the family. Don't resort to harsh methods, no matter how tempting it may seem, or how much pressure you are put to. Harsh or punitive methods of training could pose welfare issues and in general take the dog longer to learn (because pressure is not conducive to learning), and also the dog may well develop avoidance behaviours.

This is not to say that you should allow the dog to rule the roost, he should be guided into the correct behaviour and use of commands such as leave, off, sit, down and come (once taught) will help to control the dog. There may be times when it is appropriate to mimic the action of the pup's mother, by pushing and holding the dog to the floor when he has over stepped the mark but, great care should be taken, these actions should never be done in anger. In some cases it could be dangerous to advocate, for example dominant dogs could retaliate, heavy or fragile dogs could be easily injured - much discretion is needed before suggesting the use of this natural technique.

The use of stories to illustrate a point are very useful. As you progress you will build up your own repertoire of success stories and perhaps a few scenarios to illustrate how things can go wrong. If you are just starting you have my permission to steal a few of mine - there are quite a number throughout my other books and if you have been to one of my talks or courses you may be able to recall a few more.

Skills Analysis

Just as you prepare you techniques when you are training your own dog, you need to prepare a step by step approach to the teaching of your clients.

If you teach the exercise in a suitable order you will avoid mistakes. It makes sense to teach the very basic skills first. Sit, down and leave are basic building blocks for future progress but, if the handler is still struggling with controlling the lead, or has inappropriate equipment, then trying to get the dog to do a basic sit may be beyond his reach.

Skills analysis means just that; look at the skill you are teaching and break it down into segments. Think about everything that is involved and start your teaching at the very first step and then work through.

In the chapter on techniques the skill is broken down from the starting point to help you. You will also find that likely problems are identified to help you to spot them as they occur, or even better, prevent them from occurring in the first place.

Room Set Up

If left to their own devices new clients will sit where they think best. For some that will mean they come right to the front. However, others will perhaps be embarrassed by their problem dog, or even afraid that they will not be able to control it, so will try to sit by the exit in case they need to beat a hasty retreat. Therefore you must control clients in a class by meeting them at the door, especially on the first night, and assisting them to the most appropriate seat.

Your seating arrangement will depend largely on your environment. Try not to pack seats too close and arrange them so that you can see all of your clients at the same time and without having your back to anyone. For safety and practical reasons, keep seats away from doorways and especially from emergency exits. Also seats should not be placed to near heaters, selling areas and, (if you have one) the canteen.

It is important to consider your clients comfort. Think about heating, air conditioning, lighting, etc. and if necessary make adjustments as the class progresses.

Close Supervision Of Individuals

The instructor cannot watch everyone all of the time, but careful spacing will help to avoid problems.

You may have a large class, but it is important to give close supervision to all individual members. Therefore do not take on a class that is too large for you to be able to do this effectively.

One confident and experienced instructor to ten beginners is just enough. Any more than ten and the clients will not progress at a satisfactory rate, and the instructor will struggle to keep control. Less is better, most instructors will be more comfortable with six to eight in the class and the clients will benefit greatly.

A large class can work if more than one instructor is available. The way we have found this to work is for one person to take overall control and the other to work by helping individuals within the class. This way close supervision can be given. The main instructor can also give one to one help where necessary, once the class is busy practising a task.

Individual problems can be tackled during a class, particularly where the problem is a common one and you suspect that many others present may experience the same or similar problems. If you ask for a show of hands to see if any others have the same problem you will probably find many do, but perhaps don't like to say so in front of the class until the issue is out in the open and regarded as common

Using these problem solving sessions for individuals can also serve the whole class, because all will benefit from listening and a good instructor will point out that, even if they do not have the problem now, they may experience it in the future, and so fore-warned is fore-armed.

Of course the very best type of close supervision is direct one to one teaching. This is particularly beneficial if the handler has a difficult problem to deal with.

Aggression is perhaps the most obvious problem behaviour that it is best dealt with, at least to start with, on an individual basis. However, there are many other problems that need special attention, retraining programmes can be tailored for the handler and dog's needs, if time is allowed for one to one tuition.

Communication

Dress Code For Instructors

Dress and groom yourself (as well as your dog), in a smart but appropriate manner. Remember you will have to be fairly flexible to handle the dogs, so don't wear restrictive or revealing clothes. You need to keep your dignity and give off an air of professionalism in order to keep the respect and control of your class.

It is important for neither you or your dog to smell 'doggy'. The dog might just get away with it, but you most certainly won't. There are lots of sprays available for the dog, but of course regular grooming with the occasional bath are the best ways to keep the dog smelling sweet. For you the answer is easy - shower or bath every day and make sure your clothes are clean and well presented. Tidy hair, face and even nails will improve peoples' perception of you - there is much truth in the old saying 'first impressions are important'. If your hair is long it should be tied back so that it does not fall forwards when you are demonstrating with or handling a dog. All of this will make you feel more confident too.

If you are working with a team of instructors it is a great idea to have a team sweatshirt or tee-shirt that you always wear when instructing. It helps clients recognise who the instructors are and makes for ease of approach. Shirts could be simply plain, with all instructors wearing the same colour, or better still, for a small charge you can get your sweatshirts and tee-shirts personalised - perhaps with your club or dog school name or an appropriate slogan - we used to use the slogan 'Train That Dog', simple but effective. Matching trousers will round off the whole

effect and create a smart professional image.

Of course all instructors will already realise the importance of suitable footwear. Set a good example by wearing flat flexible shoes or trainers.

Name badges are also a good idea, once again it is a signal that says 'I am here to help'.

Eye Contact

Eye contact is something that is often talked about in dogs, but it is just as important in the teaching of humans. As in dogs a direct prolonged stare is a very dominant act, it can feel to the recipient embarrassing, or confrontational and it can even have sexual connotations! To avoid intimidating someone, or even if you feel intimidated by a person yourself, try to look at the face just above the eyes.

When you are talking to a group the normal duration of eye contact with an individual should be around 4 - 5 seconds. This they will feel comfortable with and they will feel that they are being involved without being confronted. If you are talking to an individual you can give between 5 and 15 seconds before looking away. Avoid your eyes darting around as this will make the person or group feel that you are not talking to them directly. Some people develop a slow blink, i.e. keeping the eyes closed for more than the norm for a blink. This gives the impression that you are not interested or don't want to be there. So analyse yourself and make sure that your eye contact communicates the right messages.

Body Language

It is most important to take up a position in the front of your group that gives you control, i.e. a superior position. The best option is to have your clients seated with you standing in the front. This immediately creates the correct hierarchy in that your clients are looking up to you. Of course once your clients are used to you and are accustomed to your control, you can choose to sit when giving theory lessons, but even so, it is best to perch on a high stool instead of taking a seat at the same level as the class. However, you should be ready to rise to accentuate control or to make a point more effectively.

At all times try to face the front. This is not always easy when you are demonstrating with a dog, but with practice you can perfect this. If you have your back to your audience, not only is it rude, but it gives them chance to talk among themselves, thus losing concentration and missing your important points.

Stand up straight with shoulders back, an upright body posture will give you a more predominant role. If the instructor is slouching against the wall, the clients will also learn sloppy ways. Assume an open, relaxed but positive stance. Don't fold you arms as this is seen as a barrier. Be careful to balance yourself and don't stand on one leg, cross your legs or lean to one side. You are aiming for a relaxed, fluid but upright posture.

Your body language must reflect what you are trying to put over to your clients in order for you to be credible. If, during the delivery of your lesson, you look down or away from your clients, clench your hands, move around too much, speak in a hesitant or obviously nervous voice, or perhaps even worse, hang on to an out of control dog, you will not be taken seriously - however accurate your information might be.

Movement is another important part of your body language. It is important to move - but this should not be over done. Movement shows enthusiasm and will give more impact. Too much movement can be very distracting and the class may end up watching instead of listening.

Your facial expression and gestures can make or break a successful class. It is important to smile easily, gesture naturally but in a non threatening way, and learn to smile under pressure. Watch out for any gestures or habits that you may have or may develop as they will be distracting. If you continually fiddle with a dog lead, clench your hands or shuffle your feet you may find yourself being observed for these mannerisms instead of for your important information.

Bringing the class to order can be done in several ways without having to shout. A meaningful walk to 'centre stage', as it were, will give the majority the hint that you are about to speak. Get the message across by taking an upright body posture, slightly leaning forward, this signals you are ready to go. Stillness from you will also make people aware that you are ready - so take up your position, stand still and wait with an expectant look on your face. Someone will soon realise and the ripple effect will spread around the class allowing you to start.

Physical contact with the client is not acceptable nowadays. There is no need to put an arm round them to reassure them, and certainly never to reprimand them. If you feel it is necessary to take their dog, for whatever reason, you should always explain what you are going to do with it and ask their permission. I hope that it goes without saying that you should never inflict any pain or cruelty on their dog. Once you take the dog lead you are legally and morally responsible for its welfare and its actions.

Voice Control

Getting your voice over 15 barking dogs and 30 chatting dog owners can be very difficult for many new instructors. There is an art in projecting your voice, it is something that you may need to practice and think consciously about in certain circumstances. Your voice is the primary way that you will get the message across so you must look after and train this important tool. The subtleties such as tones, enthusiasm, energy, resonance, expression and variety are what make you interesting to listen to.

56

The art of good voice projection is based on control of your breathing. Many years ago I trained as a singer, my wonderful teacher, (the late Marie Hogarth), used to tell us to breath from our boots and feel the breath come all the way up, through your diaphragm and then out but, under control. I do not have a loud voice but, thanks to Marie I am now able to project and can work without a microphone even in a large room.

Before you start to speak, close your mouth and take a deep breath through your nose, relax your throat, head and neck, feel the air coming up thought your lower rib cage, keep your shoulders still and then aim your voice at the furthest point. If you are standing well back so that you can see the whole of your class, they will be able to both see and hear you. Practice this art until it feels natural and you no longer have to think about it. Do not snatch breath from your stomach as this will not give you enough power to project. You will end up by coughing at your pupils. Learn to take your time and breath well.

If you are giving an instruction to a class that is already active, slowly turn your head as you speak starting at one end of the class and finishing at the other, if they are arranged in a circle turn the full circle as you speak. Enunciate the words slowly and clearly emphasising all the syllables and you should find that all will have heard enough to understand.

Are you being heard? It is good practice to ask if all can hear, but be careful that you don't do this in a raised voice and then go back to your normal voice once they have said 'yes'.

Take into consideration the acoustics of the building, partitions in the roof rafters can create a block that carries your voice to the ceiling instead of to the clients.

Pacing yourself is another important part of communication. You will find that, for most people, it is necessary to slow down from your normal speaking speed but, at the same time you should not over emphasise this.

In some instances you could use some sort of signal to inform the class that you want them to stop what they are doing and listen. I use a signal successfully with competition handlers who tend to be very noisy in their enthusiasm. A short blast on a whistle is my signal to stop. If you do use a signal don't forget to tell the clients what the signal means and your reasons for using it. I usually explain that I don't mean to be rude in the use of my whistle to stop them, but to raise my voice over the sort of noise that I do expect them to make, might result in my voice breaking down before the end of the course.

The only disadvantage in using a sound signal is that, occasionally, you may find a dog that is frightened by it.

Language

Aim to use the right level of language, appropriate to the age and ability of your clients. Be very aware that many will not understand some of the common terms used in dog training. For instance, for the new beginner to dog training, does 'Heel work' equate exactly to getting their dog to walk on a loose lead, by their side? Is a 'Recall' getting the dog back, or is it something to remember? They certainly won't have a clue what is involved in 'DC' or 'ASSD', even if given their full titles, and terms like 'sendaway' will be very confusing. It is acceptable to use terminology when it is appropriate, but explain exactly what is meant by these terms, detailing what is required by handler and dog.

Relationship with Clients

Every person that comes to your class will have their own individual set of ideas and needs. They will have certain expectations and some uncertainty about what they can and cannot achieve by being there. It is therefore important for you to assess your clients abilities, aims and desires and, whenever possible, teach to those needs. If a client's wishes are unrealistic or inappropriate these must be discussed with him, and where necessary, alternative suggestions made. This whole procedure involves you listening effectively.

To listen effectively you need to maintain an active interest in your clients. An ideal time for this is when people are arriving. There is always a staggered effect as people come into your class so take this opportunity to talk on a personal level, make friends with them and their dog and find out how they are getting on and whether anything is bothering them.

Class Position

It important that you position yourself so that all of your clients can see you and you can see them. This will mean centralising yourself and allowing space between you and the class.

If your clients are in a line in front of you, as most will be, at least to start with, stand well back. This will aid in your voice projection, and stop you inadvertently talking to those immediately in front of you. Take this opportunity to take in the whole scene and use the people and their dogs to aid and personalise your presentation.

If, once the class starts you have your pupils arranged in a circle around you, you will need to stand in the centre and turn as you speak to ensure that all are hearing everything you say. This will also mean that you are not standing continually with your back to one person. If

Stand well back from the class

the clients are already in the process of training their dogs when you need to speak, you will have to move quite smoothly but quickly. Sweep your voice around the whole circle, leaving a trail of sound to catch all their ears.

In most instances, it is best to stop the class before you give further instruction - it is very difficult for the new dog owner who is busy trying to carry out a task with a dog to listen to more instructions at the same time. They will need all of their powers of concentration for the job in hand unless what they are doing, has already become second nature to them. Of course stopping the class will also mean that there is less noise and you can be more easily heard.

If the class is arranged at random around the room, the options are to either find a place where you can be seen by all - or to move amongst them. The draw back with moving amongst the class is that it takes away your control, to a degree, i.e. you are no longer in that commanding position at the front of the class. It can be distracting for the clients because dogs will respond to you as you pass by, this will give the handler a greater degree of difficulty in controlling the dog and other handlers will no doubt be captivated by the dog and the owner's efforts to control it and forget to listen to you or loose control of their own dog! Also, once again, it leaves you with your back to some of your clients.

A good way to find a suitable position to speak from is to take up you position at one end and then ask the class to spread out making sure they can see you, you may need to help them to find a suitable place if they are shy, or have chosen a position next to an unsuitable dog but, overall the class will find their own place.

If the class is busy with an exercise, then walking amongst them and giving individual help is quite acceptable and indeed necessary. At the same time you must keep you wits about you, be fully aware of what the rest of the class are doing and be ready to deal with, or preferably prevent, any potential problems.

Homework and Handouts

Homework is a must at any level, and as the instructor, you can always identify those that have spent time doing what you suggested and those who did not.

Careful handling of the owners is needed to help them achieve the weekly aims. Do not put on so much pressure that they feel they cannot return the following week if they have not achieved. At the same time, they should be made aware that the training class is not about training the dog in class, it is about the dog owner learning in class what to do, and then putting it into practice what he/she has learnt, during the week at home. It is amazing how many pupils think that the dog will learn all it needs to, simply by attending class for six weeks!

Homework can be given in written form, and this is perhaps advisable if there is more than one thing to remember. Certainly at least some should be written, as this will emphasise in writing that homework is an important aspect of the course or class. Simple homework can be demonstrated, and then tried out in class, before the handlers go home to perfect it.

Handouts have mixed benefits. Some owners love to receive everything in writing, they thrive on taking home their instructions, information and even homework sheets, and follow everything to the letter. Others take them and never read them!

Handouts do give an air of professionalism, and also they can be worded to underline and confirm all the important aspects of training and behaviour control.

There are two main benefits; firstly to the owner - if they miss something in class they can always check it out on the handout. Even the most intelligent of people has a limited attention span, and with a lively pup to contend with, it is natural that something could be missed.

From the instructors point of view, in these days of tendency to sue, you have proof that you gave the correct and appropriate information if you have it in writing.

Make sure your written instructions are easy to follow, (try them out

on a friend first), to be on the safe side always add, 'if you don't understand, or if you are not having success, please ask in class for assistance'. Even if you think something is straight forward, it may not be so
easy or natural for the new dog owner.

It is also worth giving written recommendations of other types for
example suitable books on training or general care.

Samples for You

There are samples of handouts and homework sheets in *appendix* 1 .
These were designed by the author and used in her classes - you may
copy and use the handouts and homework sheets as long as you
acknowledge the author's copyright.

There is also a booklet available which covers basic dog training in a
little more detail, but aimed at real beginners (*see page* 216).

First Night

On the first night at class both owner and dog will be excited and nervous. There is a tendency for owners of large or boisterous dogs to slot themselves in as near to the door as possible, perhaps to make a quick exit, but it is more likely that they feel embarrassed at being dragged across the floor in front of everyone. However, sitting by the door often causes problems with other dogs coming in, so it is important to greet everyone as they arrive, and help them to find a suitable seat where they can feel reasonably in control.

Running a dog class is the same as any other business, in that the clients need to feel important, so go over and make friends with them and their dog, listen to what they have to say, ask simple questions, and make some form of complement or positive comment towards them and their dog. Knowledgeable comments based on what you see in front of you will give the owners confidence in you. Comments like; 'what a beautiful specimen', or 'I bet he keeps you busy', or 'I love crossbreeds - my first dog was a Heinz 57', or 'what a gorgeous puppy'. Try to avoid negative comments like 'what is it', or 'whatever possessed you to have one of those', or 'this breed always has problems', (even if you feel it is true!)

It is always good form to make friends with the dog; a handful of tasty titbits will help, even if the dog is too worried to take one at first, the pleasant smell will help break down the barriers.

Checking on the suitability of the dog owner's equipment is important, many will have totally the wrong things (its amazing how many pet shops manage to persuade owners to purchase huge 'Lord Major' style choke chains for little dogs). (*See Training Equipment*).

On the first night it is important to explain a little about the dog's mind and how it differs to our own, and to suggest motivations for the various individuals. The correct and safe use of titbits and toys, demonstrated by example and explanation, will help to get the owners on the right track from the start. It is always a good idea to 'show' what you mean, rather than just explaining, because a visual has much more

63

impact and is more likely to be remembered, so bring along some suitable toys and titbits to show your new students, and if appropriate try them out on some of their dogs.

You can't expect to make a great deal of progress on the first night, because dogs need time to settle and owners need to realise that they are not on their own with their problems. After a demonstration, most will be able to manage to get their dog to sit, and perhaps down and stand using a titbit lure. They will be able to practice this as homework to give them more control next week, and when next week arrives they will have achieved this task with ease, giving them the feeling that they have achieved something already - things can only get better from now on.

Puppy Classes

Puppy classes are not a new concept by any means, training clubs have been running classes for owners and their new puppies for many years. What has happened over recent years however, is that instructors have become more aware of the advantages of having a 'young puppies only' class, instead of a young dogs/puppies class, which in practice often ends up with a few more mature unruly individuals being included.

Puppy classes are essential if behaviours like this are to be controlled

In previous years, it was much more 'hit and miss' as to whether the new starters were all puppies, and often they were integrated into established groups much more quickly. The disadvantage of the old system is that it is very easy for some handlers to be lost amongst the many, and their needs not identified and dealt with. Also in the old system there was a very high fall out rate, where as when a group of owners start with their new puppies, there is more camaraderie, a genuine interest in each other's progress, a sharing of problems, and so on. Therefore, most will see through and complete a set course, (particularly if they pay in advance), and will go out from the course armed with a good starting point from which to progress. Obviously, the benefits of attending more classes should be pointed out to all students. Ideally, there should be a progressive structure within the training establishment, set up for them to follow through, to learn and achieve more as they go along. They will encounter new problems as the dog hits adolescence, then again when he/she becomes adult which perhaps they had not anticipated, or moreover, never expected would happen to them and their wonderful pup!

Class/Course Structure

The primary aim of a puppy class is to give the new dog owner an insight into some of the basic handling and management techniques, as well as some general care skills that will help them to end up with a well adjusted, easily controlled pet dog.

Occasionally you will be approached by more experienced handlers who wish to bring along their new pups for socialisation. Although the puppy pet class is not structured specifically for these, in my experience they often help by example, showing the new owners how to relax and get to know their dog. It has to be said that the majority of dogs will only ever be pet dogs, their owners may wish to aspire to more, but many give up before they really get started, having not appreciated the time and commitment required to achieve anything more. Therefore it is important to aim the class at the majority, but have the ability to be flexible, use what you have in the class to the advantage of all.

Every course should, and will, differ slightly. Owners will come with differing problems, from a variety of situations and backgrounds, and of course the breeds will vary, so you must be flexible. Having said that, you should develop a format to follow, i.e. an overall course plan, with a week by week lesson plan, otherwise you will tend to miss things out. If you don't plan ahead you will spend your free time wondering and worrying if you have covered everything you intended to cover. If something does get missed, (and it will happen, especially if owners are interactive and/or problems occur that must be dealt with there and then), it can always be carried forward to the following week. At the end of each lesson summarise to the class what you have covered, talk about its effectiveness and consider any problems that may have occurred. Make a personal note to remind yourself of any omissions from the lesson plan so that you can cover these the following week.

Age Range

A puppy class should be just that, only for puppies, but of course all breeds mature at different ages, and therefore a degree of flexibility should be applied. The lower age should be 'as soon as possible', i.e. as soon as the pup is through its inoculations. The upper age should take into consideration that in most breeds there are significant changes in behaviour between 5 and 7 months, and at the onset of puberty. Of course we would class some breeds of dogs as pups until they are 18 months or so, in particular the larger breeds, whereas fast maturing breed like the toys or even medium breeds like the Border collie, can in some cases, be quite mature by the age of six months.

The ideal starting age is around three and a half months (earlier if inoculations allow, it is worth liaising with your local vet). At around four and a half to five months, pups should be moving on to the older dog's, or better still, an intermediate class. Some dogs will benefit from a little longer in the puppy class, especially if they are of an immature or a sensitive nature. So each animal must be taken on its own merits. At the same time owners must be assured that just because the collie in their group has moved up doesn't mean they have failed to achieve if you decide to advise a few more weeks for them and their Labrador in the puppy starters class.

In well populated areas, it is possible to be quite strict regarding the ages of pups allowed on the course, in more rural areas it may not be possible to make a puppy class of this type feasible. The financial situation must of course be taken into account and small classes may not be viable. However, considering that the idea is for the pups to get social interaction with other pups, the more important factor of a puppy class is whether it is doing the intended job, i.e. are there enough people to promote worthwhile interaction amongst the pups and the people?

If you do have mixed age group classes, there are advantages and disadvantages. Of course there cannot be so much interaction between dogs particularly to start with, and temperament must be assessed much more closely, plus it is not so easy to ask owners of tiny pups to swap dogs in handling sessions and end up with a fully grown Rottweiler that they may not have the courage nor the ability to cope with. Also older dogs can be quite boisterous, even verging on the aggressive for various reasons, and therefore extreme care must be taken on integration and positioning in the room. The advantages are that the young dog can learn to accept a wide variety of other dogs and age ranges, just as he will have to in the big wide world.

Puppy Parties

There are considerable benefits but, unfortunately some dangers, in organising classes more commonly referred to as 'puppy parties'. These are for pups who have not yet completed their inoculations.

The benefits of early social and control training as well as being able to give advice to the owners are high. However, there is a health risk if pups are not yet immune to contagious diseases. If all precautions are taken, and owners are advised of the dangers and guidelines for keeping their pup healthy, these classes can be invaluable. Many vets set up their own with the help of vet nurses or local trainers. Consider speaking to your vet to see if he is interested in working with you. If you decide to do this at your own school it is still worth speaking to local vets regarding the degree of problem regarding infectious disease in your area.

Size of Class

As mentioned above, it is important that there are enough pups, preferably different types, to allow social interaction. However, if classes are kept small, it will mean that their owners will gain better and more individual help. Instructors will be able to work on more of a one to one basis, and will get to know the owners and dogs better, thus helping to identify potential problems more accurately. Ideally four, but no more than eight will be suitable for one instructor. At this level, both dog owner and instructor should feel comfortably in control. The instructor can be aware of all puppies and help to ensure that their personal needs are taken into consideration.

Once again a degree of flexibility should be adopted and if any dog or owner is not suited, or is experiencing difficulties, then the instructor should take control and move the pair to a more effective situation.

Large classes of pups, (10 plus), are not a good idea. They may provide lots of opportunities for interaction, socialisation etc., but the atmosphere is likely to be noisy. The instructor will be distracted and pulled in many directions, and it is likely that pups will learn as many bad behaviours as good, in a class that is not controlled. The lively puppies are likely to get over excited, the boisterous puppies will be very difficult to control, perhaps even developing aggressive tendencies, and the nervous puppies will shrink further into their shells.

Aim of the Puppy Class

The aim of puppy classes should be to give the owner a good start on the road to owning a well behaved and socially acceptable pet dog. The classes should be both educational and fun. Education comes in many forms; the owners may well be very naive in the science of dog owner-ship, therefore all aspects of care and control should be given, including information on how the law affects the owner and dog. Of course the primary aim is to give the owner the knowledge required to have a well controlled and sociable pet.

It is a good idea to give the owners an insight into other aspects of dog training. Most will be unaware of the many disciplines available, and will enjoy their training with added zest with the thought of a life time of fun together.

Puppy Class Instructors

Of course the instructor of the puppy class must have the same infor-mation and knowledge as any other instructor, but moreover it is impor-tant to be able to recognise potential problems and prevent them, from going any further. Many problems can be prevented from ever taking a hold if the instructor can nip them in the bud, after all that is why puppy owners come to class, they want to do what is right for their pup.

Puppies can soon learn bullying and aggressive tendencies if left to run riot in class and, although some freedom is beneficial, it should be a constructive experience. It is human nature to enjoy watching puppies playing together, and if these sessions are part of your class, owners will want them to carry on perhaps longer than you had planned, and they may try to persuade you to let the pups off more often than is good for them.

Puppy Class Techniques

With puppies, it is of paramount importance that reward based methods of training are employed. The reasons are simple; firstly these methods are easy for both dog and handler to get to grips with. Secondly they are kind and not likely to harm the dog in any way, in fact they will instil a desire to work with the owner rather than the compulsion that more physical methods can produce.

It is not uncommon for injuries to be caused to growing bones, joints and muscles with the use of more physical techniques, especially in getting the dog into the down position. I guess most instructors will have seen dogs wrestled into the down position, by means of pushing on the shoulders, using the dog's weight as counter balance, or sweep-ing his feet forward to bring him down. All of these can and do cause injury, sometimes temporary, sometimes permanent. I am not saying that all physical methods are taboo, but any used should be with extreme caution and with full care and attention to the dog's well-being.

Techniques for puppies should be based on motivation, reward and natural behaviour

Injuries can also be caused to the spine and shoulders if the 'heel - check' technique is applied for heel work. There are many better and more effective techniques that you can employ.

So it is important to choose the correct techniques to suit puppies as well as older dogs. All genuine instructors would want dogs to remain fit and healthy while under their instruction, but in these days of litigation, it is not unheard of for instructors to be sued for malpractice following the use of harsh of over physical techniques and subsequent injury to the animal. Many of these techniques have admittedly been used for years, but the connections between injury and training were not always so likely to be made as they are today.

Growl Classes

A growl class is a class that allows grumpy or aggressive dogs to come together and to learn that there is nothing to be aggressive about. The class can offer owners of maladjusted dogs the opportunity to make sense of their dogs behaviour and more importantly to gain control of it.

Setting up a growl class is not for everyone. Extreme caution and a high level of understanding is needed if the class is to be productive.

Aggression is normally exhibited by dogs who are not sure of themselves, it is a way of making things that they don't like or understand 'go away. It is, of course, also used to reprimand underdogs who push their luck. Allowing the dog to learn in a safe environment, coupled with owners modification of dominance levels at home, can very often curb if not extinguish the behaviour and give everyone a chance to relax with their dogs.

To begin with it is important to teach the owners how to control their dogs. Some basic training exercises and advice can be given before they come to class. Many dogs would not growl or be aggressive if they had more confidence in their owners. Therefore, it is important that owners feel confident in themselves and learn exercises that will help them bond with as well as take control of their dog. Social grooming, touch therapy, as well as exercises to promote owner dominance should be practised. It may also be useful to consider homeopathic treatment or Bach remedies to compliment your work.

Before coming to class, owners should know what they are letting themselves in for, and most schools have the owners sign a disclaimer in case of any problems. Of course, the disclaimer is of no use if the instructor causes a problem due to negligence, so be careful. However, problems should not occur if the situation is handled well.

When the dogs come together they should all be muzzled with secure fitting muzzles. It is advisable for the instructor to check the muzzle before allowing the handler and dog into the class.

Give the dogs plenty of space with owners sitting between dogs so that they cannot have direct conflict. In the wild or natural situation dogs would try to avoid confrontation by turning or moving away so help them to achieve this.

Training exercises can be done in the class, to keep them all occupied and most dogs will soon learn to tolerate each other.

The final step is to allow the dogs to interact. Check that the muzzles are very secure and then let a couple of dogs off to check each other out. It is probably best to allow a dog and bitch together first as any conflict is over quickly when the male realises he is with the opposite sex. It should be appreciated that, the activity in the centre of the room will have an effect on all the dogs and indeed their handlers. You may even feel your own hackles rise at the onset of any conflict. Owners should come between the two dogs to guide them away from any prolonged conflict, this is mimicking the control behaviour seen in wolves and wild dogs.

It may come as a surprise to some owners when the two dogs start to go into play behaviours, once each is allowed to check that the other poses no threat. Continued restriction on the lead in previous encounters will not have allowed the dog to get past his initial insecurity to find this more acceptable behaviour.

Of course not all dogs will end up friends, but the heat should have been taken out of the situation. Most dogs will learn to go about their own business without feeling the need to jump on top of the nearest canine.

It is a good idea to promote some physical and mental activity for these dogs, preferably an exercise that stimulates both mind and body. Working trials style training is a good idea. It couples control with activity and helps both the dog and owner focus. Some clubs build their own doggy assault course. This is a variation on agility, incorporating more difficult obstacles such as ladders to negotiate. The object is not get around fast, it is more a case of accuracy and focus.

On the down side of a class like this is the fact that you may gain a reputation for training aggressive dogs, which may result in putting others off. Also if poorly handled a growl class could end up promoting the very behaviour it is trying to curb, offering dogs the chance to practice their growls rather than find that they are not necessary, so careful planning and continuous monitoring is needed.

Even if your growl class is a great success, it should always be remembered that once a behaviour is learnt it can always reoccur. Therefore both instructors and owners should be fully aware of this throughout the dog's life.

Basic Control Training

All dog owners need to understand a little about what makes their dog do what he does - in short how his mind works. Following is a sample of how I might try to get over to owners just what is going on in that canine head and, in laymen's terms, how this affects what they should and should not do....

Laymen's Guide to The Canine Mind

One of the most important things about bringing up your dog correctly is taking care of his training. A trained dog is a pleasure to own, he will have a more enjoyable lifestyle because he will know his place, and of course can be allowed much more freedom than that of an untrained dog.

In order to get the best results it is important to make sure that your pet is fit and healthy, enjoying a good quality, suitable diet, and getting suitable exercise for his age and size. You cannot expect your dog to perform well unless he feels well. It is also important that your training is put over to the dog in a way that he can understand. To be affective at this, every dog owner should understand

What is going on the in the canine mind?
(photo by Vicky Foxton)

73

just a little about how the dog's mind works.

The dog's memory works in a different way to ours. He reacts to situations as they happen. His actions are governed by his previous experiences, his instincts, his hormones and other bodily functions. All animals and dogs are not any different, are driven by two main motivators, food and sex! It makes sense, therefore, to use one of these motivators to our advantage in the training of our faithful friend. Of course it is not easy to use sex, and therefore we look to food as the best tool.

Dogs are predatory animals, and in their development, play behaviours have a dominant role in the learning process. Therefore it follows that play can be just as good a motivator as food, if used in the correct way.

Like humans, if a dog gets too much of a good thing all but the most obsessive types will get bored or sickened. Giving controlled amounts, and just at the right time, will get the best results. Rewards must either coincide with the required action, be used as an incentive to lure the dog into the correct reaction and/or be used in a random way, for them to be an affective aid to training. For instance, if the dog is told to sit, he does so, he is allowed to move, then the reward comes after he has moved, even seconds after, the dog will associate the reward for the movement and not for the sit. This concept applies to all training, and also needs to be applied when things go wrong.

If the dog is carrying out a behaviour that you do not want, it is no use chastising him after the event. Even moments after he will no longer connect your chastisement to the incorrect behaviour. You may feel that he does understand, because he will be subdued following your chastisement, but in fact he will be reacting to your attitude, and not really understanding the reason behind it. Therefore, if your dog is doing something wrong, you should either catch him in the act, and correct him by creating either a physical barrier or by verbal command of 'No' or 'Leave', (if you have developed your training effectively), or better still, set up training situations and teach him the correct reactions in a positive way.

It is normal for dogs, just like humans, to crave for attention. Just like the child who will create a scene in the supermarket to gain the attention of a parent, so a dog will give a behaviour, whether it is desirable or not, to get a reaction from his owner. Therefore it is important to fulfil the dog's need for good quality contact and time spent together.

Having a kind and positive attitude to your training will show the dog that you are in control, and he will respect you far more than he would if your were aggressive, or lost your temper with him. Correcting behaviour is nowhere near as effective as teaching the correct behaviour in the first place - prevention is better than cure.

Using Reward and Motivation

The scenarios described above, and the starting of the basic training techniques below involve rewarding the dog when he is performing correctly. However we can teach the dog to understand the concept of receiving food or play rewards after he has performed, but he still needs to know when he is good. This can be done by teaching him that a certain sound, word or signal means he has just performed well and his reward is on its way. But, the dog has to be conditioned to this sound, word or signal in order for him to get the message. A good example of this comes in what is commonly termed 'Clicker training'. (*See clicker and target training*)

The dog's concept of a reward is anything the dog likes. Of course we cannot always use all of his choices, but even for those who are said to not like treats, there will always be something to tempt them. Freshly cooked meats are often the way to tempt even the most choosy dog. Some instructors have their own recipes - liver cake is a good economical way of making some succulent titbits go a long way in class. (*See appendix* 4)

Rewards should be given in moderation and with great care, dogs soon get fed up and even over fed by too many treats.

Some handlers have trouble moving on to competition work where rewards are not allowed in the ring, but this can be done in easy stages, kidding the dog into thinking that the reward is always there by extending the random system. (*Randomising is explained in* Clicker and Target Training). (Also, read Happy Dogs Happy Winners, *see reading list*)

Training Made Simple

Now for some simple techniques for teaching basic control that will allow most dog owners to see success in a very short space of time and give them encouragement and enthusiasm to carry on.

In each case, although there may be several techniques explained, the first one is the most preferable because it is easy and motivational. In most cases it would also be beneficial to reward the behaviour whenever it happens. For example if the dog flops down in the house the handler should give the 'down' command and reward the dog gently - being careful to not excite him and have him move. All exercises can also be trained using the clicker system, (*see clicker and target training*).

The following techniques are meant for basic training only. More advanced or competition training can be built from these starting points, but as an instructor you need to familiarise yourself with the various rules and idiosyncrasies of competition work before attempting to teach it.

There are many books written specifically for competition training and you will need to refer to these and attend competitions yourself before teaching for competition. However, more advanced work of a non competitive nature can be taught and there are a few ideas following this section.

As explained above, the easiest way to train a dog is to use a motivator. Handlers will need a supply of tiny tasty titbits, around a centimetre square which is large enough for any breed. (You may need to provide these until handlers get into the routine of using them.) The titbit must be small enough, and of a texture that will be eaten quickly.

Although high value treats are sometimes needed to get the dog started, it is best if dogs are working for the least possible reward (better rewards are saved for better performance) therefore, once the dog has the idea, you should advise the use of treats that are a little less palatable.

Handlers need to have a few titbits in their hand, and one between the thumb and finger of the same hand, this way there is always another reward waiting for the dog at the right time.

Training should always start off with the dog on lead, both in class and at home. This will help to get the dog in the right frame of mind, and of course aid control.

Have a few titbits in your hand, and one between the thumb and finger of the same hand.

76

The lead and collar should be safe, comfortable and appropriate to the size, power, and needs of the dog and the handler. (*See training equipment*)

Following each technique are ideas of '**things that go wrong**', of course you should be on the look out for others. There are some faults/problems that are common to many exercises or training sessions. One of the most common training faults is the handler making the assumption that the dog knows more than he does, or because he can 'do it at home', expecting a perfect performance in class. It is important to explain that all circumstances are different and a dog needs to be trained in lots of differing situations before he fully understands.

There will of course be handlers with some previous experience. They may have trained a dog before and will have preconceived ideas of what to do. These people may need careful handling, especially if their ideas of techniques do not match your own. Be careful to not upset them by being dictatorial, don't insist they change just for the sake of it, you may even be able to use them as an example to show others. However if the techniques used are not suitable, the dog's welfare must be taken into account and a discreet word may be necessary.

Titbits can also be a problem - whilst they are a great motivator they can be a distraction if they are dropped all over the floor, handlers need to be taught to hold one or two in their hand and have the rest in a pocket or better still a sealed container.

Many handlers will feel it natural to chastise the dog when he is not getting it right. The handler needs to be educated to understand that they are the teachers, therefore if the dog is not learning correctly they are the ones that are not getting things right and they need to look to themselves (or the instructor) for the answer.

Teaching the 'Sit'

Justification: *The sit is the easiest and most used exercise in dog training. It forms the basis of many other exercises. It is useful in control at feed times, to control jumping up and to prevent stealing. It helps to control the dog at the road side or when meeting people. It makes it easier to get the dog's lead on if he will sit. It helps with control at the vets and during grooming.*

Sit Technique One (Lure)

The titbit or toy is raised above the dog's head until he tips back into the sit position. As he does so, the keyword 'sit', is introduced in a pleasant, clear tone of voice.

The dog is rewarded while he is in position by the handler giving the

The hand position must be just right to get the dog to tip into the sit

titbit or toy. Having another titbit ready will help keep the dog in position. If using a toy the handler will have to try to hold the position by holding onto the toy a little longer.

The dog may chew at the handler's fingers for the second reward but, once he has the idea, the 'Leave' exercise can be introduced to stop this, (*covered later*).

The dog should be kept in position for a few seconds, and then the handler breaks the exercise by giving another keyword 'That'll Do'. At the same time as 'That'll do' is said, the dog is encouraged to move and the reward is stopped.

This new skill can be used and practised at various times during the day to help the handler to gain control of their dog.

Once the dog is doing the exercise competently, the keyword 'sit' should be said just before he goes into the associated action so that he gets into the routine of hearing the keyword and following it with the action.

Many short sessions are better than one long one. A good time for training is at feed time, or before the dog is allowed out of the door, in fact any time that the handler feels like 'having a go'.

Things that go wrong - Titbits all over the floor! Teach the handlers to have just two or three in their hand and the others in a pocket or container and ask them to pick up any that are dropped. If the hand position is too high it will encourage the dog to jump up.

If the hand position is too low it will encourage a down. Should the hand position be too far forward it will encourage the dog to walk forward. The hand is a moving target. All of these problems are rectified by getting the hand position right for the dog and then keeping it still - this may take a little practice with differing individuals.

Chewing on the hand/fingers often can be rectified by a slightly higher hand position to stop actual contact, or by introducing the 'leave'

78

command. Also it could be the dog has learnt that it can get a reward more easily this way, the handler may have already given many rewards without the dog having to do something for it, patience and a little explanation is needed.

Lack of interest - it could be that the reward is too bland, or not given enough to stimulate interest. It is also possible that too much has been given, this may sicken the dog. Lack of interest may be due to fear or insecurity - advise to try at home where the dog feels more confident, and/or move the handler and dog to a quieter area of class, give the dog time to take in the atmosphere before asking it to perform. Encourage the

For some dogs this hand position would be too high and would result in the dog being on his hind legs.

handler to give the dog confidence by playing, going down to dog level and holding/stroking the dog, but be careful that the handler is not rewarding a fear response - there is a fine line between confidence building and rewarding the fear response. (*See* Problem behaviours - fears and phobias).

Sit Technique Two (Modelling)

This technique requires more manipulation of the dog's body, and so the handler must be very gentle and yet firm, controlled and sure of his/her actions. The dog must be happy to be handled.

To begin with the dog should be on lead and in a confident frame of mind. The lead is held in the handler's right hand and the dog is manoeuvred so that he is on the handler's left, or if it is more comfortable, in front of the handler. The lead is coupled up and held near to the collar, or even on the collar, to give good control of the dog. The left hand is gently placed on the dog's rump and the right hand raised so that the lead is slightly up above the dog's head. This helps to angle his body into the sit position. Once the handler is competent and as the dog comes into position, the keyword 'Sit' is introduced. The dog is held there for a fraction of a second, and then the exercise is finished by the introduction of the keyword, 'That'll do', as a release command. The dog is moved off the spot by gently pulling him out of position and the reward is stopped.

Things that go wrong - The handler has too long a lead, or at least he does not take hold near enough to the dog to keep control - demonstrate again how to control the lead.

The handler pinches or pulls on the dog's skin or fur - make sure they use the flat of the hand on the dog's rump.

The dog is very body sensitive or very immature and has a tendency to wriggle away - in this case it is better to use technique one.

The dog is dominant and growls at the handler, although this is more likely when teaching the down position - dominance rules need to be applied (*See Problem behaviours - dominance*), and the training applied later when the dog has a different frame of mind.

Growling could also be due to fear - assess the dog by observing posture, attitude and questioning owner on any previous problems and the background of the dog and treat accordingly.

Sit Technique Three (Lure and Model)

It is possible and often very successful to use a combination of techniques one and two. In doing so this makes up technique three.

As before the dog should be on lead and collar and in the right frame of mind.

The lead should be in the handler's right hand, with a titbit held between thumb and finger of the same hand. The lead is shortened and help up so that it is held just six inches or so away from the dog's collar. The flat of the left hand is placed on the dog's rump and a gentle pressure pushes him down towards the sit position. At the same time the titbit can be seen by the dog, which encourages the movement. The right hand is raised up allowing the dog's nose to follow the titbit. As he reaches the sit position the handler simultaneously releases the titbit into the dog's mouth and says 'Sit'. The dog is held in position whilst he eats the titbit. The pressure on his rump is gently released but the hand is kept in position in case the dog attempts to move, the handler can then re-affirm the position. When the dog has finished the treat, he is released from the exercise as above.

Things that go wrong - Any of the problems associated with techniques one and two could occur - treat accordingly.

Sit Technique Four (Knee Push)

With a large or leggy breed like a great Dane or a greyhound the handler can run their hand and arm down the back legs, and gently push in at the back of the knee, at the same time pulling back with the lead or collar, thus hinging the dog into the sit position.

It is of course important that the handler adopts the same pleasant and controlled attitude towards the dog as in all training.

Things that go wrong - The handler finds it difficult to reach around to the back of a large dog without the head end following - it does take some practice!

Teaching the 'Down'

Justification: *This is a very important exercise, putting the dog in a submissive position, which helps in the control of dominance. It shows the dog that the handler can take the dominant position. It is useful in the home to get the dog to lie down while the owner is busy, watching TV, or eating etc. It can be used when teaching the dog to go to his bed, his kennel or his crate, or whenever additional control is needed. It is a good emergency exercise when progressed to instant downs off lead. It will be useful at the vets and when the dog is being groomed. It forms the basis of other some advanced exercises.*

Down Technique One (Lure)

Here the easiest and preferred technique uses the titbit again. This time the titbit is lowered between the dog's two front paws. It is often easier for new handlers to start with the dog in the sit position, but eventually they will be able to do this from the sit or the stand.

The hand position is adjusted slowly until the handler finds the correct position to entice the dog into the down position. Once the dog is in the down position, the new keyword 'Down' is introduced, and the dog is rewarded with the titbit. The exercise is finished as in the sit. Once the dog is doing this readily the keyword can be put in just prior to the dog going into position. This will get him used to hearing the word and to follow by doing the associated action.

If the dog is very motivated by play a toy could be used instead of a titbit.

Things that go wrong - The hand with the lure is too far forward, the dog will walk forward towards the hand, or once down crawl towards the

The titbit comes down between the two front paws

hand. Too high the dog sits. It takes practice - encourage the handler's to experiment.

Sometimes the dog's front end goes down and the back end takes a while to follow - encourage patience, the dog could be helped by pushing the back end down with the free hand, but the dog will learn more quickly if he is allowed to work it out for himself.

The dog will often push at the handler's hand, and the handler will respond by moving the titbit along the floor, usually encouraging a crawl or even making the dog get up again - the hand must be kept still, the 'leave' command can be introduced if necessary.

Handlers will sometimes release the titbit too early, but the behaviour can be shaped from there, i.e. the dog is no longer rewarded for the partial behaviour, but only when fully down.

Occasionally the dog will spring up before he is rewarded - if this happens simply advise the handler to start again and to be ready with that treat at the crucial time.

The dog could be dominant and growl at the handler as this is putting him into a position of submission and the dominant dog may take exception to this. If he does not growl at the owner he could growl at dogs around him because he feels compromised in the down, or he may simply fight the position and adopt a dominant stance (*see canine body language*) - dominance rules need to be applied (*See Problem behaviours - dominance*), and the training applied later when dog has a different frame of mind.

Growling could also be due to fear - assess the dog by observing posture and attitude and treat accordingly.

Down Technique Two (Weight Advantage)

Any physical technique to get the dog to the floor must be carried out with caution. If the dog goes down with a thud he may be bruised or even injured more severely, that is why the first technique is preferable. Also if a dog is dominant he will resist, and could become aggressive. Dominance should be tackled as a separate issue before the handler attempts to physically put the dog into a down. (*See Problem Behaviours-dominance*)

This technique works best on calmer dogs and puppies. Again the dog must be communicated with to get him in the correct frame of mind, but not too excited.

The dog is placed in the sit position using any of the appropriate techniques.

Then gentle pressure is exerted sideways on the dog's shoulder. The handler will feel the dog pushing back, when this is felt the handler changes direction using the lead to pull the dog in the opposite direction, the dog is taken sideways and downwards towards the floor and eased into down the position.

This works well especially with larger dogs. It is adopting the 'martial technique' of taking the dog in the opposite direction to the one that he is pushing, thus using his own body weight to the handler's advantage.

The dog is kept in position by control with the lead, soothing strokes, tummy tickling and calm repetition of the down command.

Things that go wrong - It is possible to bruise, strain or even damage dogs more seriously if handlers are not shown how to do this correctly. Caution should be taken that the dog is not brought down to the ground with a thud.

As with the sit the handler may not have hold of the lead correctly - usually too long.

Growling or aggression (see above). Dominance rules need to be addressed and the handler really needs to be given special tuition on how to deal with dominance.

As with the sit it is possible that growling/aggression is due to fear or even pain, therefore the whole picture should be taken into consideration before you jump to conclusions.

Down Technique Three (Hinge Back)

This technique works best starting with the dog in the stand position.

From the front, the handler places their hands at the top of the dog's legs across the chest and shoulder. The dog is then pushed gently backwards, hinging the dog back into the down position.

Things that go wrong - The dog walks backwards or sideways instead of down. Make sure the handler is pushing back and down, by holding the dog near to the shoulder and not lower down.

Down Technique Four (Sideways Push)

Similar to technique one and two the handler simply applies pressure down and sideways on the dog's shoulders, bringing the dog down on its flank. Titbits can be held down at ground level to encourage the dog down.

Things that go wrong - As technique one and two.

Down Technique Five (Barrier)

Not ideal for all handlers, if it is an appropriate technique some may need assistance. A fun technique for some, but with a serious benefit for others.

A slightly raised barrier is used to encourage the dog to come into the down position with the use of a food or toy lure/reward. The reward is placed on the opposite side of the barrier and the dog is encouraged

The handler can use their own leg to create a barrier.

to go under the barrier and down to gain the reward. The barrier could be the owner's own leg.

This technique could be used in conjunction with target training and may be especially useful for people with mobility problems.

Things that go wrong - The dog simply crawls through - make sure the reward is more obvious, and hold it until the dog is down. He tries to stand under the barrier - lower the barrier to make it more obvious to the dog.

Down Technique Six (Leg Pull)

The dog starts off in the sit and then one of the front legs is taken and pulled and the dog is pushed in the opposite direction. This is useful for smaller dogs, but not recommended for heavier or long or slender limbed dogs.

Things that go wrong - Dog goes down too heavily and injures himself. Dog learns to lift leg out of the way. Dominance problems as above.

Teaching the 'Stand'

Justification: *Needed for veterinary inspection and during grooming. The dog needs to be accustomed to being approached by others while he is standing as this will happen while out for walks. If the dog is to be entered into breed shows it will need to be happy and relaxed in the stand position. It is also a part of more advanced exercises.*

Stand Technique One (Lure)

The stand can most easily be taught, like the sit and the stand, by using the titbit method. This time the titbit needs to be in front of the dog at standing nose level. If working from the sit, the titbit is used to draw him forward into the stand by moving the titbit hand forward in line with the position that his nose will be when he is in the stand. The handler should be

The titbit must be brought up to nose height

85

instructed to stop moving their hand when the dog is standing. Watch out for those who continue to move because of course so will the dog. Reward and release as above.

Things that go wrong -The handler continues to move the hand, the dog tends to push onto the hand, and the two end up going around in circles - the hand must come to a stand still, and be held still, as soon as the dog comes into position. Sometimes the dog reaches forward without coming into the stand - the handler needs to move the hand a little quicker, but not too quick otherwise the dog looses sight of its goal. Usually the hand position needs adjusting to nose height.

Stand Technique Two (Hand Aid)

This is suitable for dogs who are happy and very confident to be handled.

The lead is held in the right hand close up to the dog's collar, the left hand is placed under the dog's body gently pushing back and up against his back legs bringing him into the stand.

Things that go wrong - The dog wriggles about - the handler probably needs to be more positive with the lift. The dog may be used to having his tummy tickled and think that this is what is happening - actually this can help to keep the dog still once he is up. Puppies often collapse to the floor and roll over - it is usually better to use technique one for most handlers and dogs.

Stand Technique Three (Foot Aid)

This is suitable for taller or older dogs. It is not suitable for dogs who have been abused or kicked at any time.

The handler needs to stand as upright as possible for this technique. The lead is held in the right hand close to the dog's collar. The handler's left foot is placed under the dog's body, and moved back towards the hind legs, then slowly and gently the dog's body is raised into the stand position.

Things that go wrong - The dog could be fearful - choose a different technique. The dog can move side ways, usually away from the handler, use a wall or other barrier to prevent the dog moving the wrong way. The dog may jump away - the handler should be instructed to make slower gentler movements. Use caution around the genitals (with male dogs in particular!) Some handlers may loose balance and could stand on the dog's foot - they need to be balanced before they start.

Putting the Sit, Down and Stand Together

Once the handler and dog can do all three positions, try teaching the handlers to link them together. Build up the time the dog is kept in each position, but remind the handlers not to become predictable. If the dog knows exactly what is coming next he will start to anticipate this, and the handler will loose the control.

Randomise the rewards, i.e. do not give a reward every time and avoid creating a pattern that the dog can follow, give extra or better rewards for progress and when the dog is obviously trying very hard to get it right.

Homework could be to repeat this, or any separate part of the exercise, whenever the handler has a spare minute.

Strengthening Exercises for Sit, Down & Stand

It is important to show handlers ways of strengthening and working on these exercises. This will also improve the handler's ability to control and work with the dog.

1 Once the dogs are stable, distractions can be gently introduced. Of course the aim is to gain success, so give your pupils instruction on what it is about to happen, and remind them how to control their dogs. It is important that they

87

become accustomed to reading their dog's body posture, eyes and attitude. They may need to shorten their leads, but make sure they are not simply restraining the animal. The difference between a tight and loose lead is a simple flick of the wrist. Be sure of your handlers and their dogs and if necessary stop distractions to help your pupils deal with their dogs.

Distractions should reflect real life, for instance another dog being walked past, a bicycle, a pram, a person with an umbrella, a ball, a child or a person using a wheelchair.

2 Another way to strengthen the positions is to have the handler put gentle pressure on the lead and at the same time repeat the keyword. This soon raises the dog's awareness of the meaning of the keyword, at least in the environment that it is being trained.

3 A third way is to have the handlers walk around their dog. To start they should only move from side to side in the dog's sight, but once he is settled they can start to move behind the dog.

Of course pupils will need to be reminded about repeating the keyword and maintaining control with the lead as well as reading body language etc.

4 Another exercise that can be done as the handler's progress is to have them arranged in a large circle or line, allowing sufficient space for another handler to weave in and out with their dog. This will also help them work on 'leave on command' and 'walking to heel'.

Impress on the handlers before they start that they must concentrate 100% on their own dog, because their dog's behaviour may change as another dog approaches and his reaction may not be the same for each dog.

If any of the dogs are particularly difficult they can still join in, but be kept to the outside until the handler has better control.

5 Homework can be to progress training to more distracting environments, but always aim for success.

Moving To Off Lead Work

Don't suddenly decide that all the dogs and owners are ready to start off lead - otherwise you could have a disaster!

1 Select one or two teams that you think will have success and have them carefully lay their leads down on the floor while the dog is kept in the chosen position, they can put their foot on the end of the lead to be safe. Keep close to these handlers and dogs in case help is needed. Remind handlers to keep repeating the appropriate keyword as they move away and remain away from the dog, using a pleasant tone to reassure the dog.

Have the handlers go back and finish the exercise after a few moments, then start it again. Advise that little and often is better than long and boring, many repetitions will help the dog to get the idea quickly.

2 Next leads can be tucked behind the dog out of his sight and training progressed as above.

3 Leads are then unclipped and immediately reattached and training put back so that the dog does not learn that as soon as hears the clip come off he can go free. Many handlers will have made this mistake when out for a walk, so the unclipping may be the signal to run riot if you are not careful.

4 Now try unclipping leads and give a little tug on the collar to remind the dog he is under control, once again just a few moments to start with.

Gradual progression with rewards for correct behaviour is what is

Holding the lead in front of the dog can fool him into thinking he is still attached if previous training is thorough

needed. I always remember my instructors saying "if your dog is breaking position you are going too far too fast".

Correcting a broken position is counter-productive as it teaches the dog that in order to get contact from his owner he should move. Even following a reprimand the dog will continue to move to gain contact, in fact in many cases it makes the dogs even more likely to break position because they become anxious and seek reassurance.

Things that go wrong -There is often someone who feels that they can progress more quickly because of work done at home - and maybe they can, but they may not get the same result in class as they do in an empty field!

Make sure handlers do not start marching off leaving dogs off lead, again they may feel that the dog can do at least the same distance as he can on lead, and the temptation is go that bit further, just to see!

General Advice To Give Handlers - Handlers should not repeat the commands without being in a position to make sure the dog follows it through, otherwise the dog is learning to ignore keywords instead of obey them.

Always train with the dog on lead until the dog is under perfect control every time.

Use opportune times to train the dog. Feed time, when out for a walk, when playing in the garden, while watching TV are all ideal. This helps the dog to understand that he can pay attention at all times not just in training school.

Little and often is better than long and boring.

Train for success.

Teaching the 'Leave'

Justification: *This is a very useful thing to teach as it has all sorts of uses. If the dog knows the meaning he can be told to 'leave' all manner of household things, slippers, the children's toys, the newspaper, even the Sunday roast! It can stop him grabbing at things he should not have, for instance, a child walks by with an ice-cream or a hot dog - if the dog understands 'leave' he can be told what to do when he is tempted in this way. It can be used if he is interested in other dogs at an inappropriate time. It is also of great use when training other exercises using titbits.*

Leave Technique One (Lead Control)

Step One - Once again start this training with the dog on his lead. A good supply of tasty titbits need to be ready.

The dog is often best started in the sit position, but this is not imperative, as long as the dog is under the control of the handler. The dog is given a titbit, with the keyword 'take it', then a second should appear between the handler's finger and thumb.

The dog is then given the keyword - 'Leave'. Voice tone should be calm and controlled, certainly not aggressive. If the dog goes forward to try to take the titbit, the handler should pull backwards on the lead, then release the pressure with a small, gentle tug, repeating the word 'Leave'. This action may need to be repeated a few times before the dog gets the message. This exercise will be of benefit to the handlers as it will help them gain better skills in timing as well as general control.

Success can be observed when the dog stops straining at the lead, or better still when

Most handlers like to start with the dog in the sit but it is not imperative - try to focus on what is being taught i.e. 'Leave'.

91

he actively withdraws. He should then be rewarded with the titbit and the keyword - 'take it' used.

The exercise should be repeated, building up in small steps and varying the time that the dog

Once step one is acheived handlers can start to put the titbit in other places, on the ground in front of the dog, even on his paw!

Feeding time is another good time to practice 'Leave'.

is required to 'leave', and the distance of the titbit.

Step Two - Once this is achieved the handlers can have fun placing the titbit on the floor and using their new found control. With each success, the next titbit is moved a little closer. Eventually the dog will leave the titbit even if it is placed on his own paw!

Homework can be to use other things that the dog likes, but is not allowed. The handler puts the item in front of the dog, controls with the lead and tells him 'Leave'. As soon as he responds correctly, he is rewarded with a titbit and the keyword 'Take it'.

Leave Technique Two (Close Hand)

Instead of pulling back with the lead as above, the handler can close their hand on the reward so that the dog cannot get to it except when he is told.

Leave Technique Three (Hand and Lead)

A combination of techniques one and two. The handler uses the lead to help control the dog, but also closes their hand on the reward.

Things that go wrong - Handlers do not read the dog's body language and fail to reward when the dog really tries - stay with the handler and point out the body language and attitude shown by the dog that tells you he is actively trying, he will look away, look at you or the handler, pull back or try to move away from the reward.

Handlers loose control of the lead, or misjudge the power needed to hold the dog back - help with distance and lead control.

Handlers reprimand the dog if he gets the treat when he should not - explain who is at fault, i.e. the handler not the dog.

The dog is not interested in the titbit - raise the value of the titbit.

Dogs grab at the handlers fingers - give the reward on an open hand, or hold the titbit in a closed fist and only open it when the dog is not grabbing.

General advice To Give Handlers - Always tell the dog to 'leave' before he has chance to touch things that the handler treasures. The dog can't be expected to know what is wanted (or not) - unless he is told!

Watch out for those times when the dog responds really well and give extra rewards at that time.

Teaching 'Walking By Your Side' (Heel)

Justification: *It is every handlers dream to have their dog walk on a loose lead without pulling their arms out of the socket. But it should not be a dream it should be a reality for your handlers. It is needed for walking the dog anywhere, whether it is for exercise, fun or necessity. It is dangerous to have a dog that does not conform to walking at your heel as it could pull the owner over, into the road, or trip the owner, (or worse someone else) up. The handler should realise that he/she may be able to hold on to the dog now, but what if the handler breaks a leg and has to use crutches, or someone else may have to walk the dog. Many families end up with just one dog walker because no one else can hold the dog.*

Walk to Heel Technique One (Mental Barrier)

To teach this effectively the handler must be very vigilant. It is a bit like sticking to a healthy diet, you must have the will power to follow it through and stick to the rules for the best results.

This first technique is one that I devised when working with college students, it is very kind to the dog and successful for those who are determined to correct/prevent the problem of pulling.

The handler decides where they want the dog to be for a comfortable position.

Step One - Training starts with the dog on lead. The handler stands next to the dog and first of all is required to work at keeping the dog on a loose lead by his/her side without moving off the spot. If they can't master this, walking will be even more difficult. So take time to perfect this first.

The handler must be encouraged to guide the dog back to them using the lead giving little fun jerks (not heavy negative checks) to reel them in, and have a pleasant attitude with verbal praise and/or a titbit when the dog is in the correct place, (ignore him when he is not).

What goes wrong? - Watch out for those handlers that simply hang on to a tight lead giving the impression that the dog is under control. Show them how to bring the dog to their side and then slacken the lead so that the dog feels no tension around his neck. (The same applies if the dog is on harness or head collar.)

Step Two - The handler should be looking to control the dog by their side in what would be a comfortable position if the dog were being walked. To achieve this ask the handler to look down and note the dog's head position.

The next stage is to add a little humour - I always liken this to a child's TV programme, 'you have to use your imagination'. Imagine just

94

in front of the dog is a brick wall. If the dog pulls forward he will damage his head!

Step Three - The handler takes a step forward, concentrating on the dog all the time, if the dog goes forward and does not stop in time to save his head from the brick wall, the handler should be encouraged to react quickly to save him!

To 'save him' - the handler stops, starts walking backwards, and guides the dog back towards and to the side of themselves with the lead. The dog should be kept on the same side that he started. The handler should keep guiding the dog until he goes past and behind them. Then, the handler must start to walk forward again, this will encourage the dog to turn, follow, and come back to the handler's side. When he is back at the handler's side they should continue forward. If the dog goes forward from the desired position, the procedure is repeated.

When the handler starts to move forward the dog will too. But most dogs have naturally faster pace than humans, so most will end up ahead of the handler.

What goes wrong? - Handlers turn around instead of going backwards, some handlers (about one in 15) find walking backwards difficult, usually it can be mastered with individual help. Many allow the dog to go too far forward before going backwards, this is particularly so when they start to get a little success or if they are used to the dog pulling hard, again individual help can be given by the instructor walking at the handler's side and pointing out the times to react.

Keywords - It is not necessary to introduce any verbal commands, until the dog is getting the idea, just a few murmurs of encouragement as he comes towards the handler, and again when he comes into position, but nothing when he is incorrect.

The handler starts walking backwards, and guides the dog back towards and to the side of themselves with the lead

Voice control is important, many handlers tend to want to chat away to the dog, or give commands, but if the handler gives verbal reward or commands as the dog comes into position, it is very easy to be still praising or commanding as he walks past and goes forward into the wrong position again. It is better to remain silent until the dog is looking up for approval in the right place.

The dog is then encouraged into the correct heel position.

When he is correct he is rewarded with praise and possibly a titbit.

Demonstration is a good way of getting this over. Use an instructor's dog, or a carefully selected clients dog, and emphasise the fact that it can all be done without a word being spoken. Dogs pick up on the body language very quickly, especially if the normally noisy handler suddenly goes quiet!

If the dog is considered by the handler to be head strong, perhaps dominant, or has simply learnt the wrong habits too well, the handler will have to be extra determined at this stage. Speak to these handlers separately, or when teaching one to one, put more emphasis on this and explain that the dog has had plenty of time to learn the wrong way, so they must be determined.

Of course the instructor may also have to emphasise the importance of maintaining a pleasant, controlled manner, handlers soon become frustrated if they think that their dog is more of a problem than others.

Soon, with the handler's perseverance, encouragement and support from the instructor, the dog will get the message and will be walking happily by the owner's side.

Walk to Heel Technique Two (Titbit & Barrier)

The above technique can be followed, with the added aid of a titbit in the hand, on the side that the dog is walking, so that the dog comes into the correct position, he is greeted with an immediate reward.

Things that go wrong - As technique one. Also, the titbit is held in the wrong position, usually across the handler's body or wide of the handler, and so this is where the dog ends up. Advise to keep the titbit at the handler's side.

Walk to Heel Technique Three (Titbit Lure)

Sometimes it is sufficient to simply use a titbit as a lure to get the dog to follow at the heel position. The titbit is held on the side that the dog is to work on (usually the left). It is kept at the position that the handler requires the dog's nose to be when they are walking. Periodically titbits are given, but it is important that the handler is in control of their rewards. The teaching of 'leave' will help this. After a while the handler starts to reward from the opposite hand so that the emphasis is taken away from simply following a lure.

Things that go wrong - As technique two

Walk to Heel Technique Four (Toy Lure)

As three, but using a toy to reward and lure the dog. The choice of toy will alter the ease of control, and will be dependent on the dog and handler. A toy that both the handler and the dog can hold may be beneficial, but once again the handler must be in control of the reward.

Walking to Heel Technique Five (One Step Patience)

This technique relies on the dog working out for himself what it is the handler wants and is similar to technique one except the handler is not required to walk backwards - and some really do struggle with that. This is a very effective technique but, as with all techniques, it requires patience from the handler.

The dog is on lead and the handler stands still giving little fun tugs on the lead to stop the dog relying on leaning into the lead.

Once the lead is slack the handler can move forward, if the lead goes tight or the dog bounds forward, the handler should once again stand still, hold the lead still, and then follow up by repeating the process of tugging him in until he is on a slack lead again. It should be emphasised that the tugs are not hard checks and the dog should not be subjected to harsh treatment. A hard check, particularly when he is taken unawares, could cause serious damage to his neck or spine.

Walking to Heel Technique Six (Targeting)

The dog can learn to walk to heel very effectively using target training. This is similar to using the titbit or toy lure, but the dog is conditioned to a specific target. (*See clicker and target training*).

The tip of the stick is used to lure the dog's head into the required position for a perfect exercise and then he is rewarded using the clicker training system.

This is a very effective technique with food lovers. Even the most boisterous can soon become focused and will be walking on a loose lead with a minimum of effort. The effort comes in the conditioning before hand.

Problems with this?

The handler has difficulty with the length of target, a smaller one will be better for this, especially for tall dogs.

The new or inexperienced handler has trouble enough with the dog without having other gadgets in their hands.

Moving to Off Lead Work

As in the static positions, it is not a good idea to suddenly say to a class full of pupils "now we start off lead work". Select a few handlers and start them off by having them make sure they can work with the lead loose all the time. Then they can tuck the lead in a pocket. Make sure they continue to use all other aids to maintain the dog in the heel position.

Once success is gained, the lead can be unsnapped and reattached as in the static exercises, (sit, down and stand), before you advise the lead being taken off. Once again gradual progression and not with the whole class at the same time.

General advice to give handlers - It is normal for dogs to pull forward when being walked, especially as they mature, because their natural pace is faster than that of humans. Therefore it is something that the dog will have to work hard to achieve as well as the handler.

There will be times, even after the dog has learned what the handler wants, when the dog will start to pull forward again. For instance when the dog is excited or in a new environment. The handler needs to learn to identify these times, and be prepared to work on control.

It is important that the handler gains control at a 'stand' first - this will give him/her confidence and the dog will be starting to take the right approach from the start.

Make sure the dog is rewarded for the correct behaviour - do not fall into the trap of ignoring the dog when he is working well and only reacting when he goes wrong.

If the handler doesn't want their dog to pull, they will have to decide to prevent it all the time, not just some of the time. Alternatively the dog can be taught to pull on command.

Teaching The Dog To 'Come Back '

Justification: Dogs that won't come back can be a danger to others and certainly a great cause of frustration to their owners. The dog needs to understand an instant recall from the garden, other dogs, things he should leave alone, strangers, visitors, when out in the park or countryside. An instant recall could save the dog's life.

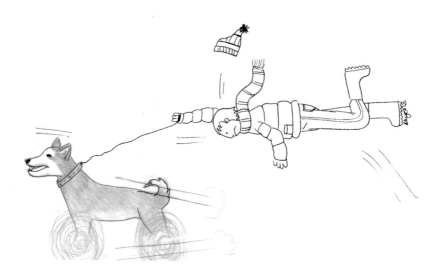

'Come' Technique One (Titbit Recall)

The dog is on lead, he is shown a titbit and then given it. At the same time the handler says the dog's name and the keyword 'Come'. He does not have to move for the food the handler is simply teaching him that the keyword 'Come' means he will get a food reward if he is in the right place and paying attention to his owner.

Next take a step away encouraging the dog to follow and hold out the titbit and repeat his name and the word 'Come'. This time he is given two titbits because the dog actually made an effort to come towards the handler.

Next the handler moves away a little more, still encouraging the dog, as he returns from a greater distance the stakes are increased to three titbits this time.

This can be repeated often and the reward increased when the distance is greater and for quick responses. But, don't keep building up the amount of food three repetitions is enough for one session.

The handler's body posture can push the dog back and make him worried about approaching even for his favourite reward.

Things that go wrong - The handler tries off lead before the dog is conditioned.

The titbits are uninteresting, dropped, remain the same, too many or too little.

Also the handler's body posture may be oppressive to the dog. Advise handlers to stand up as straight as possible or to bend at the knees rather that at the waist.

'Come' Technique Two (Motivation recall)

If the dog likes playing with toys or enjoys his food, then this can be put to the handler's advantage.

The handler should be made aware of the value of toys, but also the problems associated with dominance and of course complacency. They should make sure that toys are not always available to the dog. In fact toys should be put away in a drawer or cupboard, and brought out only when the handler wants to play with the dog.

Step One - The handler needs to decide which toy the dog likes best, and keep this as the 'special toy'. (A squeaky toy is great for this exercise, because it has an audible attraction too).

The exercise should be started in a quiet place, the garden perhaps, where the handler can play with the dog and the toy without fear of interruption or too much distraction.

Step Two - The dog can be kept on lead so that he has no alternative but to come to the handler when he is called, this helps to eliminate unwanted behaviours like running in the opposite direction with the prize!

The toy should be thrown a few feet, and then the handler encourages the dog to retrieve the toy. The dog is reeled in, the handler repeating the dog's name and the keyword 'Come', giving tiny fun jerks on the lead, and portraying an enthusiastic attitude. If the dog does not hold onto the toy this is not a problem, the handler simply goes to the toy and rewards the dog by playing, the dog will soon learn that this is fun.

Step Three - The handler should be encouraged to repeat this procedure often.

Step Four - When the dog is enthusiastically coming to the handler, the sit command can be introduced. Start off by simply getting the handler to couple the two exercises together, i.e. when the dog comes the handler then goes into the sit exercise.

Step Five - Now instead of just getting the dog to sit, encourage the handler to touch the dog's collar before he gives his reward, then the dog should be allowed to go free again.

The toy or treat can be used to encourage the dog into the sit position

Now each time the dog comes and sits, the handler can follow this through - touching his collar and then rewarding. The dog will soon learn that coming back to the owner results in reward and not the end of his fun. (Previously he may have come to understand that each time the

102

owner went for his collar it meant that the lead would go on and it would be the end of the fun).

Step Six - Once all of this is achieved the handler can start from the beginning, but off lead. The exercise should be taken step by step in a controlled safe environment until it is certain the dog is always happy to come back instantly when called.

Step Seven - Once he is confidently and enthusiastically coming, the handler needs to change the place that they are training so that the dog gets the idea that the same applies in varying environments. At first the area should not involve too many distractions, and the handler should be encouraged to play with the dog, and not become too formal or dictatorial. It important that the dog is called back and has fun with the handler. He can even be rewarded with the occasional delicious titbit to heighten the enthusiasm.

'Come ' Technique Three (Long Line recall)

A length of line will help the handler keep control and yet still give the dog some freedom. He will also learn an important lesson - the handler is in control of his freedom!

This technique is especially advantageous for use on dogs that have already learnt to 'not' come back.

Use a long line - twenty to thirty feet long, attached to the dog's collar. (A washing line is cheap and ideal for this, but you can buy extending leads or tracking lines). Now the handler has complete control and can call him and reel the lead in as described in technique one.

The owner should observe body language, and indeed if running off has been a problem they should be able to easily notice the first signs. When the dog shows the signs that indicate he is about to run off, the handler should immediately call the dog back using the line, before he has chance to try, so that the dog starts to realise that the behaviour of running of is no longer an option.

As the dog's behaviour gets better, gradually cut off sections, making the line shorter all of the time. The dog will associate his new good behaviour with the line, and the last few feet should remain attached to the dog for quite some time to be sure of the correct association.

'Come' Technique Four (Hide and Seek Recall)

This works especially well with pups or less confident dogs, and is something handlers can do when out for walks in a safe environment. When the dog is preoccupied the handler can run away, down wind of the dog, and hide. The dog will realise that the handler is missing and panic a little, he may well rush around trying to find his owner. After a little while, if the dog has not found the owner, he should appear and call the dog using his name and keyword 'Come'. When the dog gets to handler - lots of fuss, a food reward and a game. This should be followed up with several call backs to reinforce the learning. The dog will learn to keep the handler in sight at all times and will be observed checking.

'Come' Technique Five (Chase Me Recall)

Here the handler is encouraged to run away from the dog - calling his name and using the keyword 'Come'. After a little way the dog must be allowed to catch up and then rewarded. It works in a similar way to technique three.

'Come' Technique Six (Restriction Recall)

This can be done in class or the handler could set it up with a friend. The dog is held while the handler runs away from the dog. The handler turns and calls the dog in an enthusiastic tone. The dog will be motivated to return because of the restriction and of course the handler running. (*See photo opposite*).

'Come' Technique Seven (Distraction Recall)

Here we teach the dog to come back from distractions. The handler deliberately walks forwards and allows the dog to interact with a distraction, another dog, a tree or a person etc. Then the dog is called using his name and the keyword 'Come', reeled in with the lead and rewarded.

When the dog starts to respond well by turning as soon as he hears his name the rewards are increased. The handler then learns to give big rewards for excellent recalls and lesser rewards for okay recalls.

'Come' Technique Eight (Puppy Recall)

This incorporates the heel work. The handler walks with the dog at heel and then backs off and calls the dog towards him, using the dog's name

and the keyword 'Come'. The lead is reeled in and to start with the dog is rewarded for simply coming to the handler, but later the sit can be introduced. Although this technique is generally referred to as the 'puppy recall', it is an excellent strengthening exercise for dogs of any age.

Moving To Off Lead Work

The same principles of teaching apply as they did with sit, down and stand off lead. Gradual progression, not the whole class all together, help the handlers train for success.

Make sure handlers continue to positively reinforce every part of the exercise.

Dogs can be rewarded by freedom itself and in the recall exercise this is

The instructor holds the dog and then the handler makes it attractive for the dog to want to come back (technique six).

especially true. If all dogs are of sound temperament, and the handler is taught how to gain their dog's attention, selected dogs can be off lead, called back to the handler and then sent back to play with other dogs, as in technique seven. This is an exercise best started with young dogs. It should not be allowed to develop into a free for all, you must work on the handlers to make sure they work hard on their dogs.

General Advice To Give Handlers - Body posture and eye contact can have a big influence on the dog's attitude to recall. If the handler is facing the dog, bending forward or over the dog or looking directly at him he is less likely to want to come. Handlers should try looking to the side and let the dog see them actually move their head to the side. They should try bending at the knees and have an open posture. Signs from the dog that he is unsure will be circling the handler, reacting to the call but then sniffing the ground or finding something 'important' to do. Often a simple turn of the handler's head is all it takes to bring the dog in!

Voice can also be off putting, particularly deep gruff sounds.

With all techniques for teaching the 'Come', times when the dog is enthusiastic about being with the handler can be utilised to encourage the dog to 'Come', for example feeding time, walkies time etc.

The handler should be reminded, never to chastise the dog for not coming back because, when he does come back, he is doing the required behaviour, even if it is after he has been called for a long time. Rewards for this delayed reaction can be limited to a stroke on the head, but the dog should not be punished in any way.

The handler should not be content to see the dog running off on his own. Excursions should be teamwork and fun for both the dog and handler. The good dog handler has lots of games along the way, then coming back will not be seen by the dog or indeed the handler as a chore or even a punishment.

Never run towards the dog to get him to come back - always move away. If handlers run towards the dog he will simply keep going in the same direction as the handler.

The responsible dog owner should be aware of what is going on around them all the time. If a stray dog (or even an accompanied dog) enters the park, the handler's dog should be under control and not running towards the other dog. If children are playing or other people are enjoying the environment the responsible dog owner does not allow their dog to interfere with their enjoyment. It should be remembered that not everyone loves or even likes dogs, some are afraid and should not be put in a compromising position.

Be safe rather than sorry - if in doubt have the dog on lead. Extending leads can give freedom and preserve sanity during training if used in a sensible manner, (*see training equipment*).

Teaching The Dog Not To Barge Through Doorways

Justification: *It is dangerous to allow the dog to barge through doorways. The dog may push someone over, charge out to challenge a visitor or, if he is on lead, pull the handler through with him. He may even damage himself or cause an accident. The handler going into new environments first is also a dominant act, therefore it helps to get the message across that the handler is the boss.*

All dogs need to learn not to barge through the dog before the handler.

Ideally you need a false doorway set up in class, but if this can't be done use an imaginary doorway - a line on the floor, a couple of markers, even a couple of stones will give the handler a barrier to work to. An internal doorway could also be used as a starter. Using an external door is possible and of course this is what the handler is working towards, but most will find this very difficult to start with.

Step One - The handler needs to be set up fairly close to the doorway, because if they are too far away they will not be able to go through the doorway while still maintaining control of the dog's lead at the other side.

Step Two - Instruct the handler to hold the dog back with the lead, and keep relaxing the lead a little and then tightening it with an upwards movement, until the dog stays back at the given point. The easiest word to use is 'Wait'.

It does not matter if the dog is in a sit, down, or stand as long as he is under control. Some handlers may gain this control by incorporating a certain position, but make sure that if they are for instance telling the dog to sit, that they follow this through and keep the dog in a sit until it is time to move.

Step Three - As soon as the dog is observed actively trying to keep position, the handler should go back and reward him and then start again, thus enforcing this part of the exercise.

Step Four - Once the dog is stable, i.e. not trying to pull forward, the handler is instructed to repeat the keyword 'Wait'. Then the dog can be called through the gap to the handler. The handler should be careful not to allow the dog to lunge forward - it is better to bring the dog into a sit, or have the handler walk off with the dog at heel, depending on their experience. If this can't be achieved then use some form of lure to make sure the dog goes directly to the handler.

Step Five - Once the dog can be controlled through an open gap, you can take the handler on to an actual door. Start as above, then with full concentration on the dog. They must reach forward to open the door a little, still holding the lead in an upwards position to control the dog, repeating keyword, 'wait'.

If the dog lunges forward towards the door, the handler should close it and start again.

Step Six - Once the dog is good at all the above, the handler needs to change doors and start again at step one.

Step Seven - At home the handler can keep changing doors until all are successfully mastered.

General Advice: Handlers can start to incorporate the training without the lead on internal doors at home so that the dog understands that this is something that must be done both on and off lead.

Internal doors are much easier than external doors so always advise to start on these first.

Don't cheat - it is easy to call the dog through when he has already started to move of his own accord. Even if he was just about to be called he should be put back into the 'wait' position. Then the handler can go back and reward the 'wait'. Handlers should be encouraged to be sure of the dog's stability before calling him.

Teaching 'Don't Jump Up'

Justification: *This an extremely important exercise for any dog, but even more so with a large dog. If the dog jumps up it may very easily knock someone over - probably the handler, but worse someone who is not accustomed to dogs.*

The handler may not mind the dog jumping up but should be reminded that the dog cannot differentiate between clothes that don't matter and the handler's best going out clothes. If it is accustomed to jumping up it will do so indiscriminately and may cause injury.

'Don't Jump Up' Technique One (Using Rewards)

When teaching a puppy, the owner should always go down to the dog's level to give praise and cuddles, never letting the dog jump up to be rewarded by stroking or any form of contact or reaction.

If the pup does jump up, the handler should stand up straight and if necessary, turn their back on the dog withdrawing all contact. Then the handler should face the dog again, remembering to be patient. Keep quiet (any verbal or physical contact is self rewarding) wait until the dog behaves more appropriately - most will sit eventually - then the dog can be verbally and physically rewarded in a calm manner.

Control the dog on a lead and get the visitor to reward when the dog is sitting.

'Don't Jump Up' Technique Two (Control & reward)

If the dog understands the keywords it can be told to 'Sit' when it approaches. The use of a titbit and/or if the dog is starting to understand a hand signal will help him into position. This is followed up with reward (praise strokes and cuddles), but only when he has all four feet on the ground. If he tries to raise up again the handler should withdraw and/or repeat the sit command and signal.

If the dog jumps up when the owner comes home after being away from him, they should be instructed to have a titbit ready and to insist on a sit before the dog gets any attention.

Visitors to the home can be asked to do the same. The handler should control the dog on lead when visitors arrive. The dog should be made to sit before he is allowed to say "Hello".

'Don't Jump Up' Technique Three (Lead Control)

The situation is best set up by the handler or to start with in class. Allow the dog into a situation where he is likely to jump up and then the lead is used to control the dog, the handler pulls firmly downwards and away from their body.

This technique can also be used to stop the dog jumping up at visitors and others. If the dog is allowed to jump up it is really too late to train using this technique, although the handler could go into technique one or two. The contact the dog gains is self rewarding.

General Advice To Give Handlers - The handler should never let the dog jump up and then make the mistake of rewarding by stroking or giving any form of contact or reaction.

Handlers should be advised to not leave training until dressed in their Sunday best, or great aunt Audrey is coming to stay! Prevention is better than cure - preparation is a must.

The handler should always try to be in full control of the inappropriate behaviour, this will speed up the learning process.

Other Training Activities

As well as the exercises that will teach the dog and handler basic control, the good dog school also prepares the clients for life style occurances. For example dogs should be trained how to react amongst crowds, in conjunction with traffic, cycles, joggers, wheelchairs, prams and so on. Sometimes it is a good idea to take your class outside of the usual environment so that you are on hand to help them cope in changing circumstances. They will enjoy it too.

These students were taken, with their dogs, to a picnic area to socialise and to learn how to behave in a new environment.

Taking the dog and the children is an everyday occurrence for parents, the instructor can help them to make this a pleasant experience rather than a chore

More Advanced Training

As with all exercises it is best if you, as the instructor, teach at least one of your own dogs to do these exercises before embarking on the teaching of others. After that, plan out the steps and then perhaps begin by teaching a friend so that you can get your procedure and teaching technique right.

Also, it is worth checking out whether the handler you are teaching wishes to take part in open competitions or whether they are training just for fun as this may affect your approach.

In this section is a brief description of what is involved and some guidance on how to start the exercises off for beginners. However, it is advisable for you to get some expert tuition, before trying to teach any degree of precision or depth. If you do not get a good depth of understanding, you will create mistakes for those who wish to be competitive. Always choose experts who use motivation and reward based techniques.

Teaching retrieve is always useful and fun

Teaching The Retrieve

Justification: *Retrieve is a fun exercise to teach the dog and it will help to exercise him. It can also be useful if the handler wants something picking up, and it forms the basis of searching which can be useful if the handler looses their keys in the park. It is also a competition exercise.*

Retrieve Technique One (Motivation)

Step One - The handler should chose an article that the dog will like such as a play toy, a tug rope etc. The handler should commence by enticing the dog to take hold of the toy by waving it around along the floor, or in front of the dog, just beyond his reach.

Once the dog is stimulated by the toy, he should be encouraged to go forward to take it. The handler praises the dog and then takes the article, before the dog has time to wonder what he is supposed to do next. Once the article has been taken from the dog's mouth, immediate calm and quiet is necessary. If the handler carries on praising after the article has been taken, the dog will start to spit out the article instead of retrieving to hand. He may even refuse to pick articles up in the future, associating praise at the end of the exercise as the thing that he is rewarded for. It is human nature to praise after the event, but handlers must learn to think like a dog, and you must listen out for their mistakes as they may not realise they are making them.

This first stage can be practised at home ready to progress when at the next session

Step Two - When the dog is confident in taking the article, the handler can introduce the recall by calling the dog, using the keyword 'Come', gently guiding the dog with the lead, collecting it up as he comes. Then when the dog is with the handler the article is taken from his mouth.

Remind the handler not to yank the lead as the dog may drop the article.

The amount of time that the article is in the dog's mouth should be minimal, seconds only, not allowing time for the dog to start any chewing as this could be a problem if the handler wants to go on to competition work.

Step Three - Keywords - To begin with it is best to say nothing to the dog, except maybe to make a few exciting sounds to motivate him but, once the dog and handler have gained some success, introduce the word 'Hold' as the dog goes forward and takes the article.

Step Four - Depending on the type of dog, and what the handler is wanting to achieve from the exercise, you can now help them to make a progression. It is sometimes appropriate to introduce the control element, i.e. the sit prior to going out. This is normally the next stage for a very attentive and keen dog. All the components of the recall can be used in this exercise to gain better control.

If the handler has been keeping the article in their hand, they can now get the article nearer and nearer to the ground. Progress no more than a few inches at a time, and going only as fast as the dog remains confident.

Retrieve Technique Two (Motivation Plus!)

Sometimes dogs are just not that interested in retrieving, even though they will quite readily play. If the dog is food motivated, then this can be used to teach him to retrieve.

The same procedures can be followed, as above, but the handler should substitute the article for something that the dog can smell, has food in it, but will not be easily broken by the dog. For a soft mouthed dog a Smartie tube, or bag tightly wrapped with treats in it will be suitable. If the dog has a harder bite then use a more solid tube or packet.

The dog does not necessarily have to get his reward directly from the packet although, if this can be arranged, it works very well. As long as the dog can't take the food himself it will work. The follow on is as in technique three (incentive).

Retrieve Technique Three (Incentive)

This technique is great with food oriented dogs, it shapes the dog's behaviour but the handler must be both vigilant and patient. It is ideal for dogs that have the start of a retrieve that needs perfecting, particularly good for dogs that tend to drop the article in front of the handler. It can also be used to teach a dog from the beginning (*See shaping*).

The handler will need to keep some food in a container that is easily opened, to reward the dog.

The handler must aim to reward the dog very quickly as he brings in the article, but the dog must learn that the handler takes the article and then he gets the reward. If not the dog will soon get into the habit of spitting out the article, in order to eat his treat.

It is crucial that he soon starts to associate the keyword 'Hold' with reward. If he does drop the article before the handler can take it, the dog should not be rewarded, instead the handler should make a point of returning the reward to its pot, and then start again.

It is useful to have the pot of treats on a chair or table at the handler's side. The dog can then see the reward, and can also see when he is not rewarded, as this becomes far more obvious to him if the treats are out in the open.

Here we are using the shaping technique, ignoring incorrect behaviour and rewarding correct behaviour, building up his retrieve, by incentive, a little at a time.

As the dog progresses the rewards are given for that little bit more effort, to encourage when the dog is unsure, or even for a small step forward. The dog soon starts to eliminate the behaviours which do not get the reward.

Teaching Retrieve Over A Hurdle

The dog must be old enough, and well developed physically, before training can start. Train on lead to start with.

The handler needs to teach the dog to go over a hurdle as a separate exercise first.

Step One - Begin with a very low hurdle, say 6" from the ground and get the handler to jump over with the dog.

Throwing his toy over and allowing him to run forward will also help him to be enthusiastic and will aid the retrieve.

Step Two - Once the dog is happily going over, introduce the keyword for jump, 'Over', the word should come in just as he is about to lift into the jump.

Step Three - The next stage is to teach the dog to go over on his own. First the handler should stand between the dog and the jump, but to the side, and encourage him over, guiding with the lead, and using a toy to encourage.

The distance can slowly be increased, until the handler can stand at the side of the jump, looking at the dog from the other side. Again guide with the lead so that the option to do anything other than jump is minimal.

If the dog tries to go around the hurdle to collect his toy, get the handler to throw the toy over and go with him a few times to eliminate that behaviour.

Step Four - At this stage of training the dog probably already knows the static sit position so, if he is stable, the handler can leave him in the sit, go over the jump themselves, and then call the dog over. The handler can use his lead to guide the dog and prevent him from going in the wrong direction.

Step Five - Once the dog is confident, we can introduce the return. This should be relatively easy. The handler positions themselves at the right hand side of the jump. The dog is placed in the sit position, (on lead) facing the jump, and to the handler's left. The dog's toy is then thrown over the jump, the dog is sent over to collect his toy and as he goes over the jump, the handler repositions to the front of the jump, ready to call the dog as he turns with his toy. The lead is still on to guide the dog back over the jump.

It may be advantageous to have another toy to encourage the dog back.

A short cut is to teach the dog in an area where the only option to get back is over the jump. In a corridor for instance, or over a fence. This works very well as a basic teaching principle.

Use the lead to guide the dog the first time any new hurdle or new article is introduced, to make sure that the dog understands what is wanted.

Sendaway

Teaching The Sendaway

Justification: *The sendaway is great fun for both dog and handler. The object of the exercise is for the dog to go to a specific place. It is useful for sending the dog to his bed, or to teach him to go to a certain place. It is also a competition exercise.*

Sendaway Technique One (Play Drive Motivation)

Step One - Play is the basis of this method. The handler needs to get the dog really motivated onto an article.

Step Two - The next step is for the handler to show the dog the article, stretching out their arm, fanning backwards in a circular movement, enticing the dog to run in a circle, forward and towards the toy.

The object of the exercise is to get the dog looking in the direction that the handler is pointing. At this stage the dog will actually be going around in a circle, but this doesn't matter. The important factor is that he is enjoying going towards the motivator and making an association with the pointing hand.

Step Three - Once the dog is looking intently in the direction the handler is pointing introduce the keyword 'Look'.

Step Four - Next introduce the sendaway command. Common keywords used are, 'Go' or 'Away'. The dog is held back with his lead. The handler needs to stand forward of, and sideways to the dog, with the toy in their outstretched right hand. When he is looking the keyword 'Look' is given, and then when the dog is raring to go, the keyword 'Go' is given and the dog is allowed to run towards the article and is rewarded with it.

Step Five - Now introduce a fast down. To get a good down the dog must understand that, in order to get his reward, he must go down immediately he hears the keyword 'Down'. To ensure this, the training is quite specific.

Start at the beginning with the motivator, but then as the dog is going around at a decent speed introduce the 'Down'. To do this, the motivator is brought down to the floor, just ahead of the dog. The action should be carried out with urgency and excitement but not aggression.

The handler should try to keep the toy covered by their hand. The dog is then stopped in his tracks by halting the hand holding the lead and dropping it to the floor. Then the handler must swiftly move that same hand to the dog's back, just at the base of his shoulders, to help push him into the down. It may be necessary to run the hand down to his rump to push it over because some dogs halt in the play mode, i.e. bottom in the air.

This is followed up by the releasing of the reward between the dog's two front feet whilst he stays in the down.

Once the handler is confident, introduce the keyword for dropping the dog. 'Down'. Do not overdo the instant down training for the first few sessions as this may result in a reluctance to 'Go' .

Step Six - The next stage is to build a little distance and encourage the dog to go. This is done by placing the motivator just a few feet away, and then the handler goes with the dog, who is kept on the lead of course.

Gradually increase the distance a step at a time. The further the distance, the greater the chance of things going wrong, so be very care-ful and sure that the dog is confident before progressing. Be sure that the dog is going into the down on the keyword, and prior to getting the reward, before much distance is allowed because the handler will not be able to control it.

Step Seven - If the dog is good and stable in the static sit, more progression can be made. The motivator article is placed about two metres away, then the handler stands with the toy, but to the side, facing the toy. The dog is given his 'Look' word to get his attention onto the area, (and the handler points to where he is to go), followed by his 'Sendaway' word. The dog is encouraged towards the area by the handler patting the floor or waving the toy to motivate him. The handler is in position to make sure the dog goes into an instant down, before he is rewarded. Thus, he is now going to the designated area, on his own.

Step Eight - Once this is accomplished the handler can progress the distance, back towards the dog, step by step, until eventually the handler can stand with the dog and send him. The progression must be gradual and the dog must be kept well motivated all the time.

Sendaway Technique Two (Food Incentive)

Start as above, but instead of a toy use titbits. The titbits should be kept in a container that the dog can see but cannot access on his own. The treats are in a tin to stop the dog sniffing around and loosing concentration.

It is a good idea to have some titbits in the tin and some in the hand. The handler needs to get to the titbits quickly in order to keep up the momentum, and the dog must think that they came from the tin in order to be sufficiently motivated but, sometimes it is easier to cheat a bit. So long as the dog knows (thinks) that treats come out of the tin, and that he gets one when the tin is in the handler's hand then the method will work.

Teaching The Dog To Search for the Owner's Article

Justification: This is a fun exercise that can help with fitness. It also has a useful aspect if you loose something the dog can be sent to search for it. The handler can also progress to scent discrimination or area search in competition work.

Step One - Ideally this is started at home or out in the field. The handler needs to find an article that the dog likes, e.g. a toy, a ragger, a knotted sock etc. Then the dog is encouraged to retrieve it.

Step Two - Once a simple retrieve is accomplished the article is hidden in an easy to find place. It is often best to throw the article behind a chair or into some long grass so that the dog can see the direction it went. Then the dog is encouraged to find it. The handler should go along with the dog to give him confidence and enter into the game. The dog will soon come to associate the keyword 'Find' with using his eyes and hopefully his nose to find the article. Hiding the article in long grass will encourage the dog to use his nose.

Step Three - The dog should be encouraged to take scent from the handler's hand. This is simple - the handler puts their hand in front of the dog. The dog will naturally move forward to smell it, this is then coupled with the search keyword, e.g. 'Find'.

Step Four - Once the dog is competent the handler can try other articles. They should always start off with a game so that the article is familiar and fun, this will motivate him to hunt for it.

Step Five - When the dog is very confident the handler can start to use articles that the dog has not already been allowed to see, touch or smell. Once a successful scent has been achieved the dog should once again be encouraged to play with the article.

In class you can get handlers to put their articles on the floor and get the dog to find their own amongst others. (Start with immovable objects plus the handler's object to be sure of success.) If the basics are followed this can very quickly be successful and it gives owners a great sense of achievement.

Teaching Tracking For Fun

Tracking is a rather time consuming exercise. You need to go to an area suitable for tracking i.e. grass or farm land that is relatively free from people walking on it at least in the 24 hours before you do the exercise.

Despite its logistical difficulties, it is a great exercise to teach. Many handlers have great fun and you may find that even difficult dogs can become very focused on this. It should be taught in a fun, yet constructive way.

Although dogs are normally tracked using a harness and line, it is acceptable to start new beginners on a basic flat collar and lead. The track is laid by the handler who drags a toy along the ground or scuffs their feet leaving a trail from the starting point of a tracking pole. A further pole can be placed at the end of the track to help the beginner know where they have been and the toy left there as a reward. Then the handler/track layer comes back along the same path. Usually the dog is held by the instructor or another helper, sometimes it is better to get the owner to hold the dog while the helper or instructor lays the track. With larger groups it is a good idea to pair handlers so that they help each other, training one dog at a time and putting the other away in their car or tying him up.

Once the track is laid, the dog is allowed and encouraged to follow the track. The handler points down to the ground and encourages the dog to follow the trail with his nose, he is rewarded at the end with his toy and a good game which involves the handler and the toy. A short track starts them off, (around 12 feet), but after a few sessions, length and degree of difficulty can be gradually extended. The addition of corners, really starts to give the owner a buzz because it then becomes very obvious that the dog is following the track rather than just pulling forwards.

Additional articles can be laid along the track and the dog is encouraged to pick these up too. If the dog is not motivated by toys food can be used, but it is best in small containers so that it is easily found.

Tracking

General Advice - It is best to lay tracks with your back to the wind when the dog is new to tracking. If the track is laid with a cross wind, dogs tend to drift to the side picking up the scent in the air rather than on the ground.

When laying the track, look ahead, mark a point on the horizon and walk towards it so that you are walking in a straight line.

Keep close to the pole as you start so that the dog is not sent wide of the track at the beginning.

If more than one person is working at the same time make sure there is plenty of distance between them, it is probably better to let one person go at a time.

Teaching Agility For Fun

Agility is very popular and many handlers enjoy having a go just for fun, it is a good way of giving clients something to progress to, once they have some basic control. It is simple to teach, but rather costly to set up.

Points To Consider

Safety - Make sure the equipment you use is strong and safe, always test it before every session to be certain. Consider the weight and size of all dogs who are to be involved, a dog walk that holds a Border collie may not be so safe with a Leonberger on it! Be aware that even though equipment should have non slip surfaces, it may be more dangerous in wet weather. After regular use, non slip surfaces may become worn, and loose their grip. If the dogs don't slip the handlers may loose their footing on slippery grass. Equipment must be well maintained and kept in good working order.

The equipment that the handler uses on the dog should also be taken into consideration. It is normal to start handlers and dogs new to agility on lead, but be careful. It is easy to catch the lead on the equipment, this may result in the dog being worried, but worse, it may pull equipment down or the dog off the equipment.

Slip leads are the most common for agility because they are easily taken off and on but, to start with, any soft lead and collar are suitable. A reasonable length to the lead is needed. 48" plus will allow the handler to manoeuvre around the equipment.

It is a good idea to get handlers to work in pairs when starting out, putting one dog away and together working on one dog at a time, they can help each other on the high equipment. Also, the tunnels are far easier if the handler can call the dog from the opposite end while their partner holds on to the dog at the start of the tunnel.

On high equipment make sure an instructor is available to help even when handlers work in two's, a third pair of hands to steady the see saw, assist over the top of the 'A' frame, and to watch the dog's back end on the dog walk, will make the whole exercise safer and aid in the confidence of the dog and his handler.

The Dog - It is important that the dog is fit, the correct weight for his type, fully developed physically, and under good basic control before you allow the handler to embark on agility training. Also make sure long coated dogs can see where they are going and are not stepping on a trailing coat.

Take the training very slowly and selectively to begin with. For the dog to do the whole circuit, using muscles he is not accustomed to using will be akin to the handler spending an unaccustomed hour at a keep fit class. The next day he will know about it through his aching muscles! Of course jumping takes a lot out of a dog, but also clambering up the 'A' frame, dog walk and see saw takes a lot of strength and stamina.

If handlers are enthusiastic, but the dog is not too fit or still quite young, handlers can start by having the 'dog walk' dismantled and on the floor or raised up on a couple of blocks. Jumps can be started at just a few inches high, and handlers can also use natural obstacles when out on walks, for example fallen branches. However, the handler must be warned to only do one or two jumps at each session. The tunnels are fun and safe even for very young puppies.

The Handler - Although it is not important whether the handler is an athlete or not, at least at the fun level, they should be able to control the dog, be capable of supporting it on the high equipment and be suitably dressed, i.e. in flexible clothing and wearing flat shoes, walking boots or trainers (if the ground is dry). If the handler is disabled in some way it may still be possible for them to take part, but careful thought and support must be given to make sure that both the handler and the dog are safe.

General Advice - On contact equipment (A Frame, dog walk and seesaw) titbits or toys can be used to encourage the dog along, but handlers must be careful to keep the lure on the equipment and not in the air - the dog needs to have his head down looking at where he is going.

Teaching Flyball For Fun

Another great sport and fun for all. Flyball involves the dog catching and retrieving a tennis ball from a 'flyball box'. In a competition it is a team event with dogs jumping 4 hurdles, hitting the box, retrieving the ball and returning over the hurdles to the handler. Hurdles are usually low but, under some rules, the height is determined by the shoulder height of the smallest dog in the team. In others the height is the same for all, (12" in the UK). The fastest team wins.

Flyball

The dog needs first to be able to paw, retrieve a ball, jump a hurdle and recall to its owner. These can all be taught separately. Retrieve, hurdle and recall we have already covered. The paw is simple and most dogs pick this up quickly. The handler simply holds something, preferably the ball, in their hand, or better still under a board or similar flat surface. The dog is tempted by the handler and as soon as it makes any attempt with its paw, to get to the ball or treat, the handler releases it.

Once this is achieved it is a simple matter of shaping the paw behaviour to give more power to gain its reward. This is then transferred to the box, the training board can be put on the box to start with to help the dog.

It may be necessary, at the beginning, to help the dog to trigger the box by releasing the ball from inside, but don't be afraid to let the dog work things out for himself.

Some dog are a little worried by the noise of the box triggering the release of the ball. If this happens get the handler to play with their dog near to the box while you or a helper release the trigger a few times. Usually dogs get over this initial fear quickly because the whole concept is motivational.

The hurdles are taught separately, using a ball to encourage the dog over and back. Careful positioning of the handler will help to ensure that the dog comes back over the hurdle with the ball.

When adding more hurdles start with the last hurdle first, i.e. the one nearest the box, and then very gradually add hurdles in front.

Fun Activities

It is so important to keep dog training fun. For many going onto the precession of competition style obedience will be just too intense and they will lack the enthusiasm and motivation to train to this degree. However, introducing some of the more advanced exercises as explained in the previous chapter, and/or some fun activities will keep your clients coming back for more.

First of all there are things that you can arrange such as fun days, parties, photo sessions or demonstrations. Speakers of all types go down well including: vets, holistic experts, dog wardens and groomers. You can give short lectures on topical issues, organise general socials, quizzes, dog shows, walks, keep fit for dogs, dancing with dogs/heel work to music, formation obedience, fast sit competitions, swap dogs, retrieves from water, find the lead, musical chairs and road work. Even the simple raffle sparks of interest but, remember, you need a licence from the council to run raffles and the like.

Some activities can take up a whole evening or even a day, others can be part of the ordinary session. Some activities could include, for example, a prize for the best trick each week, or the best exercise performed that night, the most improved and so on

I have attended some great fun days. The instructors and organisers put on some entertaining events such as a mock show, a sausage race, a picnic and perhaps a teach in on something new - clicker training can be fun. These events need not cost too much, prizes can be treats for the dog and a key ring or other small momento for the handlers. Food can be supplied by the clients - ask them all to bring something and have a general buffet table or alternatively they bring their own picnic packing up.

Alternatively you can have a more serious side to the fun by having competitions, progress tests or even better organise something like the KC's 'Good Citizen Test'. People can then work towards this, but are not under any pressure to take part if they don't feel ready. This can be coupled with some fun events so that there is something for everyone to do.

At Bishop Burton College we organise an annual competition that gives all students
of dog training something to aim for.

Clicker and Target Training

Clicker training follows the Skinnerian theory of 'operant conditioning'. The concept is one of the most successful tools a trainer can have. If you once understand and use the system you can train to a very high standard. The clicker is a sound signal but you could use all manner of other things. Some trainers have used whistles in the same way. You could in fact use words as signals, but the beauty of a clicker is that it always sounds the same, it never gets angry or sarcastic!

The first step in clicker training is to establish a signal. The signal should mean to the dog "food/reward is coming". The reason for establishing a signal is because simply giving a food reward during a desired behaviour is sometimes difficult, therefore a signal like the sound of a clicker becomes a secondary reinforcer, and the animal is conditioned to understand that this will lead to the primary reinforcer or goal - usually food or a favourite toy/game.

To give an example of why the concept works; if a dog retrieves and is then rewarded how does he know which part of the exercise you are pleased with? He may think that all parts are good and get hung up in a fixed pattern of behaviour which holds both errors and accuracy's. He may also get there slowly by trial and error. Physical correction is undesirable and indeed counterproductive - it is so easy for the dog to make a connection with the wrong part or even the whole exercise and be put off totally, therefore a positive signal is the best way of getting your message across - the exercise or parts of it can be rewarded while it is in progress. You can strengthen small responses, leave undesirable responses unrewarded and even correct behaviours by good use of a well conditioned signal.

Conditioning The Dog

It is a good idea to get into a routine when training. This induces anticipation and heightens the dog's willingness to work. The trainers appearance with a bag containing all the training aids will be sufficient to get the dog into the right frame of mind after just a few repetitions.

Some dogs even go looking for the equipment when they know a session is about to start.

It may be necessary at the beginning to use a very succulent reward to get the dog in the right mode but, once this is established and the dog is switched on, rewards can be varied and the favourite titbits given for the better responses.

The dog needs to learn that when he hears the sound of the clicker - food is coming.

The first thing to teach the dog is that when he hears the sound of the clicker a titbit or favourite toy/game will follow: So click the clicker and give a reward in sequence until the dog has the idea - Click - titbit, click - titbit, click - titbit and so on until dog responds well

Next start to put in a time gap: Click - few seconds gap then titbit. Gradually start to extend the gap up to 30 seconds or so.

Once this has been done vary the time lapse. This randomisation is important because without this the dog will start to learn a pattern. It is quite difficult for people to achieve because we find it easier to have a set structure to our behaviour.

Random reinforcement is more powerful than a fixed schedule of reward. A human example that illustrates this is if you can imagine having a car that gives you difficulties each morning trying to get it started, but eventually it starts so you always keep trying. If you were used to the ease of starting you would be inclined to give up much more quickly.

Now it is time to alter the circumstances. As with all training the dog needs to learn that the exercise is not specific to this environment only. It will be necessary to start at the beginning as if the dog did not know the concept to be sure that he understands fully. Then remember to keep rewards randomised. Don't fall into those pattern forming habits.

Applying Clicker/Signal To Training

Once the dog is conditioned to the sound of the clicker you can start to use it.

The first rule of 'operant conditioning' is to be sure of what you are reinforcing. What you reinforce can be based on what the dog does naturally, or you can induce a behaviour in order to reward it. It can be real fun waiting for a dog to give a behaviour and once the dog gets into the concept he will start trying out the repertoire of behaviours to see which one meets with your 'click' of approval. It is a good idea to start off training a behaviour that you don't see as important, therefore you will not be worried about making mistakes - perhaps a new trick is a fun way to get to grips with the concept.

So, induce or wait for a desired response - then signal, i.e. click the clicker and follow this up with a reward. To begin with the reward comes straight away, once the behaviour is stable you can start to vary the time between click and reward, but the click must be given as soon as the desired behaviour is seen.

Keep repeating until animal is correct each time and ignore any incorrect behaviours that are given. Apply the random schedule to reward when the behaviour is stable.

Occasionally, when the dog does exceptionally well or makes a real effort towards the desired response give a double reward i.e. extra treats or a special ration. The dog soon starts to try to work out what it is that gets the special treatment.

If things don't progress you need to ask yourself why? It may be necessary to alter the circumstances to induce the correct response. It could be that the dog has not really got the idea, it may be that what you are asking is beyond the dog's mental or physical capabilities at this time.

If you are adding to an exercise or trying to improve it in some way you may have to drop or relax other criteria in favour of rewarding the new part. Then, once this is achieved go back to basics to re-establish the rest of the exercise.

Remember what you are doing is 'shaping' behaviour, i.e. taking a behaviour gradually towards the perfect goal. Scientist call this 'successive approximation'.

Providing you can figure out a way of breaking down the behaviour into steps you can use shaping to get almost any animal to do anything that it is physically and mentally capable of. Shaping is used by trainers of cetaceans i.e. dolphins, whales, spinners, porpoise etc., also by circus trainers who are involved with elephants and large cats etc.

A good way of getting to grips with the concept is to think about the way dolphin trainers get the dolphin to jump through the hoop. They couldn't pick him up and throw him could they?! Therefore they use a succession of approximations, gradually getting nearer to the desired goal.

Getting Behaviours Under Command

This is technically referred to as 'getting behaviour under stimulus control'. We will give a 'cue' to the dog that means he should give a set behaviour, for example the keyword 'sit' would be a cue for the dog to sit.

The first step, as before, is to get the dog interested by the trainers appearance with the reward, training bag etc.

Then introduce the word or signal you want to use, click and reward when the dog performs correctly.

Stop both the command and the reward. Take a break of about 30 seconds and then repeat and reward for correct behaviour. If the dog does the behaviour and you have not given the command or signal ignore the behaviour.

Dogs may initially perform 'off cue' in an exaggerated way. This is normally a sign of the dog starting to understand. Soon he will perform more 'on cue', and the lack of reward will gradually extinguish 'off cue' behaviour down to its naturally occurring level.

Extending, Improving and Chaining Behaviours

To get a dog to do a longer exercise, e.g. a 'sit' for a few minutes instead of seconds is relatively easy. Simply get the dog into position but do not click immediately. Wait a few seconds then click. Gradually build up the time before clicking. Make sure that this build up is gradual and remember that some dogs will have shorter attention spans than others.

However, dogs can learn two concepts in clicker training; (1) the click means 'good dog and end of exercise' and (2) the click means 'keep going that's good'. When starting out usually the former is the case, but as behaviours become motivational in themselves, parts of behaviours are chained together and coupled with the dog's greater understanding of random reward, the dog can learn to keep going and be encouraged by the sound of the click.

To start off chaining (linking) behaviours together you need to always train each element separately, teaching the final element first if possible. Once the final element is trained go on to the penultimate part. Once this is accomplished link the two by introducing the final element cue (keyword or signal) and when the dog has performed click and reward.

Once the dog has made the link the command or signal (cue) can be given on approach to the penultimate part. However, if the cue is given too early the dog will skip and go to the end because he is accustomed to getting the reward at this point. This, perhaps, helps to explain the amount of anticipation in competitive dogs.

What To Do When Things Go Wrong

Occasionally dogs who know what to do will fool around or refuse to give a desired behaviour. We can issue punishment using this system. The punishment is not of a physical type, but never the less is quite severe, so you must only issue this if you are absolutely sure that the dog truly understands. To be sure of this ask yourself this question - 'has the dog performed this behaviour in a variety of circumstances, including this one, on a least 20 occasions? Has anything happened to make him unsure of himself? Does his body posture and behaviour appear confident?' If the answer is yes to all of this then the dog may well be just choosing not to do as you ask, therefore you may be justified in issuing a punishment.

If your dog enjoys training the worst punishment is to take the opportunity to train away. (The Americans call this 'Time Out'). If he has been conditioned correctly to start with he will be devastated and try much harder to keep in your favour in future.

So, to issue punishment the first thing to do is to withdraw all rewards. That includes your attention, pack up your things and leave training area, leaving the dog behind.

Leave him alone for 2 -3 minutes. Then re-appear with the rewards. Repeat the command given earlier. In most cases the dog will respond favourably. Reward his good behaviour with the clicker and food reward.

Occasionally the dog will not respond, in this case repeat your actions. If this still does not work abandon the session and start again another time. Take time out to consider what the dog understands and what he does not. It is still possible that he is confused. If this is the case start the training process again.

Target Training

The principles used in clicker training can be applied when teaching target training. This is where the dog follows and touches a target to get the reward.

In actual fact our hands are targets when we use the lure method of teaching the sit, down and stand. The dog follows and touches to get the titbit.

It is a good idea to use some form of pointer that can act as an extension to your arm, this will be a more positive sign to the dog too. Traditionally this is a black stick with a white end, referred to as a target stick. A good alternative that fits in your pocket is a telescopic pointer pen as used by lecturers and teachers to point to things on the board.

The clicker conditioned dog will soon get the idea of touching the end of the stick with his nose. Simply set up the training with some favourite rewards, and show the dog the stick. Most dogs will be curious and will sniff at it, as soon as this happens click and reward.

Often within minutes the dog has the idea. However with some dogs it does take a little longer. Once the dog has the idea you can give this a command. 'Touch'. Apply the 'on cue' - 'off cue' training, as in clicker training, until he touches only when told.

Vary the environment and training position. Once the behaviour is

The dog learns to touch a target stick with his nose

stable, you can start to use it to draw the dog into behaviours you might want. A good start it to get the dog to put his paws on something (a low table or chair) using the target stick to lure him. Once you have achieved this you will be ready to progress to teaching all manner of things - it is great fun.

It is easy to transfer the training to other targets too, for example in FCI obedience the dog has to go to a cone and stand, target training is great for teaching this, simply teach the dog that the cone is the target.

It is easy to teach the dog to recognise other items as targets.

Training Equipment and Aids

There is an ever increasing variety of equipment on the market for dog training. Many items are excellent, some of course, are not so good. As all intuitive instructors know, it is not what equipment you have on the dog that matters, it is what you do with that equipment that makes the difference. Most competent forward thinking instructors and handlers prefer to opt for comfort all round, both for the dog and for the handler.

In this section I have undertaken to describe and evaluate the many differing types of equipment that all instructors should be aware of, even though they may not necessarily use all of them. There are some items described in this section, the use of which I hope instructors reading this book will never advocate.

Collars

Buckled Collars - Suitable for all breeds, definitely for pups, giving gentle guidance and restraint. As we go to press, buckled collars are probably the most popular means of restraint used by dog trainers who are keen on positive reinforcement/reward based training. If dogs are trained correctly this is likely to be the only means of restraint (plus a lead) they will ever need, apart from when taking part in specialist activities like tracking etc.

Made of a variety of materials, the best are strong fabric such as cotton, nylon web or good quality bridle leather. Some buckled collars are made with a ring at the end, (sometimes called a goat collar). These are exceptionally secure as the strain is placed on the end of the collar where it has several layers of material/leather, instead of the side which only has one layer.

The only real draw back is that even if quite close fitting, some dogs can easily back out of buckled collars.

Half Check Collars - (Sometimes referred to as collie collars). These give a central pull for guidance, correction and restraint. More secure than buckled collars for large or boisterous dogs because they close up when the dog pulls in any direction, therefore the dog is less likely to be able to back out of them. The half check gives added control without the harshness of choke/check chains.

Like buckled collars, they are made of fabric or leather, usually with the linking circle made of chain, although it can be made of fabric or leather. They come in various widths and lengths and can be adjustable.

Choke/Check Chains - Traditional training and restraint aid, these are thankfully much less popular nowadays because negative reinforcement techniques are required for effective use.

Possible problems can occur, even from the correct use of this collar. Vets have reported dislocation and damage of vertebrae as a result of the checking action needed to train the dog. Also many owners experience coat loss due to the continual rubbing of the chain.

Available in chrome plated, brass or stainless steel, various weights, lengths and links. It is also possible to get the same design in a range of fabrics, leather and rope.

Fitted Collars - These are used like a check/choke, but fitted high on the neck, behind the ears, for better control. Minimal force is required and the dog can be guided using this system. However, it is possible to damage the dog since the collar can easily be misused in the same way, if not worse than the check/choke chain.

Usually made of fabric or rope - sometimes leather, they are available in various widths, lengths and can be adjustable.

Head Collars - Designed to guide the head to achieve control. Used by some handlers solely as a restraint but, should be used as part of

training programme to teach control for best effect. The head collar is a good quick way to give handlers control and confidence. Handler needs advice on how to accustom the dog to the head collar, giving it good associations with reward based conditioning. The head collar closes the dog's mouth as it pulls into it, so it is effective as a muzzle (while the lead is attached).

Head collars are usually made of flat nylon web, some have padding to ease any friction. Occasionally they are made from rope.

Problems - often incorrectly fitted or sold by retailers without fitting. Bad fit may result in rubbing around the eyes. Problems may also occur with the public image, the head collar appears, to the uninitiated, like a muzzle.

Electric Collar - Designed to give electric shocks while the handler is away from the dog by a remote control or other device. It is a deterrent used by some to deal with stock chasing, straying etc. There is another type that sets off the shock when the dog barks, and yet another that relates to a wire placed as a barrier, so creating an invisible fence, i.e. the collar is activated if the dog goes over the barrier.

Problems - With the remote control set, perfect timing is needed for effective use, other wise the dog may make incorrect associations which can result in fear of people or places. With all types the dog can make the association with the situation rather than its own behaviour. It is possible that other frequencies can set the collar off - mobile phones for instance.

No UK professional dog training organisation promotes the use of these collars by the general public. It is generally accepted that the risks out weigh the benefits. Use of this collar rightfully raises many welfare and moral issues. It could be said of this and other negative reinforcement equipment that, only a trainer with excellent timing and a good all round ability to read dogs should use one, and such trainers are good enough not to need one.

Sound Collars - These collars emit irritating clicking sound, controlled by a remote handler control like the electric collars.

Perfect timing is required for effective use. May be harmful to sensitive dogs. Incorrect associations may be made.

Pincher/Spiked/Pronged Collar - Metal pronged collar, prongs facing into the dog. The collar pinches the dog's skin around the neck as he pulls, or is pulled.

Perfect timing is needed for effective use. These collars are easily misused resulting at best in the dog learning incorrect associations. Many are still used on the continent and USA, but thankfully they are becoming less popular as trainers are learning more about kinder motivational methods. Use of this could well result in a welfare issue.

Citronella Collar - Works on vibration from the dog's throat when barking. The collar emits the smell of the harmless oil citronella, every time the dog barks. The idea being to control and prevent barking. Some people report excellent success others less so, overall it would seem that it works with varying degrees of effectiveness depending on the dogs sensitivity to it. Other variations are available.

Harness

Walking Harness - Designed to take the strain on the chest and shoulders, instead of around neck. Effective for some dogs with a good training programme incorporated. Some dogs (usually larger boisterous individuals) are more difficult to control on these harnesses, while others turn into little angels! These harness's are ideal for dogs who are

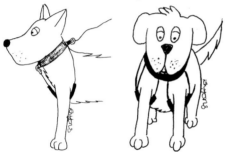

particularly sensitivity around the neck. Also where previous training methods have been abused.

Problems - possible rubbing around top of legs often due to incorrect use or fitting.

Usually made from nylon web or rope. Most now have padding around the leg area to help prevent chafing

Standard Harness - Designed purely as a restraint. If fitted correctly, the harness is comfortable for the dog and an effective restraint, without risk of neck/vertebrae injury.

Usually made of leather, but sometimes fabric (flat webbing).

Problems - it is not so easy to control the dog from the centre of his body which is were the lead attaches.

Working Harness - Various types used for sports such as water work, search and rescue, tracking, draught, racing, guidance etc.

Made from a variety of fabrics depending on the purpose and design. Fabrics include: leather, nylon and cotton webbing, sheep skin etc.

Problems - mostly due to incorrect fit. Always fit the harness to the dog before purchase or send accurate measurements if ordering made to measure. Enlist the help of an expert in the sport to help prevent any problems.

Car Harness - Used for safety restraint in the car and is attached to the seat belt.

Usually made from nylon web.

Problems - only caused by handler not getting the dog used to the harness and restraint before driving off.

Leads

General Training Lead - Usually around 48″ long, with a trigger hook fastener and ring in the handle for off lead work. Some trainers advocate longer (6′) leads for the progression to static exercises. Other trainers prefer shorter leads to maintain better control. Training leads come in varying widths depending on size of dog and the owner's preference.

Sometimes the lead can incorporate a tug toy, or the actual lead can be used as a tug, by more advanced/competitive trainers. Differing hooks are available, but the trigger hook style is generally recommended for training and safety.

Made from leather, cotton web, rope or nylon web.

Police Lead - Double training lead with two hooks and two rings, used for altering the length, and tethering. 3/4″ or 1″ x 72″. Traditionally used by police forces and some working trials enthusiasts.

Made from bridle leather (sometimes cotton web).

Useful lead but rather cumbersome, many handlers struggle to handle all of this lead. Not ideal for close work such as competitive obedience.

Guide Dog Lead - Used by guide dog owners and trainers, but also some other trainers because of the useful size and adaptability.

Made the same as the police style but smaller, 1/2″ or 5/8″ x 60″.

More easy to handle than the police lead but still rather cumbersome.

House Lead - Inexpensive rope or web line made without a handle. This is designed to be left on the dog in the home. It gives the owner better and more instant control when a training or behaviour problem occurs. However, it is not just used for solving problems, it can also be used to help train any desired response.

Gundog style lead

Problems - can be chewed by the dog.

Gundog Lead - An all in one lead and collar which allows easy on and off for working dogs. It is used for agility training and can be used in general dog training. The lead is adjusted with a rubber stop which prevents movement once in place, this means it can be positioned high on the neck, giving ease of control. The rubber stopper prevents the dog backing out in a similar way to the fitted collar described above.

Made from 3 ply or braided rope with rubber or leather stopper.

Problems - like the fitted collar and choke/check collar, it could be misused. Sometimes tightened too much.

Chain - Chain leads are mainly sold to the general pet market as 'good, strong, non-chew lead'. Made from varying gauges of chain usually with leather handle, but sometimes webbing. They are available as a choke style or standard lead with hook fitting.

Problems - they are not an ideal training lead. They are harsh on the hands and can be noisy for sound sensitive dogs.

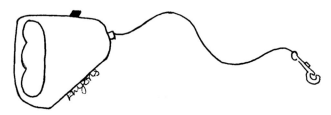

Extending Lead - This lead extends and retracts into a comfortable moulded handle. It gives the dog freedom, while still on lead. The lead can be set at varying lengths or left to go in and out as the dog moves. If used correctly, a useful training and control device. Extending leads come in varying lengths and strengths depending on desired use and size of dog.

Problems - Some owners misuse these leads by leaving the dog to wander at will in public areas. Sometimes the dog is allowed to wind around obstacles or people.

Long Lines - Often home made from a washing line or similar. Long lines are ideal when used to aid recall training, they can be shortened by cutting as the dog becomes more competent and under owner control.

Problems - they have a tendency to get wrapped around obstacles, so these are best used in open spaces. The dog or handler may get tangled in the line. The line can burn the handler's hands if the dog is allowed to run and the line whips through their hands.

Tracking Lines - Long lines used for allowing the dog to work forward of the handler to follow a scent trail.

Usually made from rope but also can be web or leather.

Problems - see long lines.

Muzzles

Basket style muzzle

Plastic Basket Style - Easily washed this style allows good air flow and prevents biting or chewing.

Problems - prevents eating and drinking.

Nylon - Open ended, nylon muzzles allow drinking and panting, therefore they are ideal for unattended dogs, to prevent chewing.

Problems - can become wet from saliva. Does not allow for heavy panting.

Leather - Basic 'stop bite' box or strap style muzzle. The muzzle is completely enclosed (except for ventilation holes) to prevent the dog biting.

Problems- prevents eating and drinking.

Metal Racing - Used for greyhounds who are traditionally muzzled for racing and while in any public area.

Dumb-bells and Dummies

Dumb-bells - Plastic or wood these are used for competitive obedience and working trials retrieve tests. In some countries heavy metal dumb-bells are used in competition. Floating dumb-bells also available but, these are generally used for fun training rather than serious competition.

Dummies - Made from canvas and either filled with sawdust, sand or both, giving differing weights for gundog retrieves. Also plastic floating dummies are available.

Toys

There are a huge variety of toys on the market, below is just a small selection of the more common ones used in training.

The general advice is; never leave a toy with an unattended dog unless the toy has been specifically designed for the purpose, and even then common sense must prevail. Always control games and toys to help in the overall control of the dog and to aid the use of the toy as a motivator.

Balls - Balls obviously come in many sizes and many materials, but for use with dogs they must be safe. Solid balls are dangerous unless suitably large for the dog, because they can get lodged in the throat and are almost impossible to get free. Hollow tennis or squeaky balls are safer as they can be easily collapsed if they do become lodged in the dog's throat, and therefore it is easier to get them out. Balls should not be left with an unattended dog.

Tug-a-balls - These are a toy comprising of a ball on the end of a short rope. They are much safer than  ordinary balls because the rope handle prevents the ball becoming irretrievably lodged in the dog's throat. They can be easily thrown long distances. Sometimes made entirely of rope (tug-a-knot), but usually rubber ball on the end of a rope handle. They come in a variety of sizes.

Problems - they should not be left with an unattended dog as they could be chewed and are not designed to be safe for this purpose.

Squeaky Toys - Available in all sorts of sizes shapes and a variety of materials. They fit easily into the pocket, and are great for gaining attention and motivation. Ideal for dogs low in prey drive as the noise helps to excite them. Of course dogs high in prey drive will love them even more.

Problems - they should not be left with an unattended dog, even those toys marked non toxic, if chewed, will not do the dog any good. Some dogs easily get the squeak devise out of the toy, this could be dangerous if swallowed. Some dogs make a lot of noise with the toy and this can be distracting for the owner and others close by.

Pulls and Rings - Tug games should always be controlled and won by the handler, but pulls and rings are great team building toys.

Pulls and rings are generally made of rubber and are strong and durable. Some made of rope.

Problems - should not be left with an unattended dog unless designed for the purpose. Could invite dominance if the dog wins too many games from the handler.

Frisbees - A good exerciser but, caution is needed. The dog jumps for the toy and in so doing may twist his back or injure his legs. Frisbees should not be left with an unattended dog, unless specifically designed as a chew toy.

Rope Tugs - Rope knotted at either end leaving tassels. Some are designed to be a pacifier or dental floss and can be left with the dog. Prey drive dogs like the tug to be moved so that they can chase it.

Problems - As pulls.

Cube/play ball - Cube or ball designed for food to be incorporated within the toy, the food drops out at irregular intervals as the dog plays with the toy. The idea is that the dog is kept amused for long periods of time because of the random reward system that this toy incorporates. Designed to be left with most dogs and being made from heavy duty plastic it is very durable.

Hollow Toys - Dense rubber, often hive shaped, this toy couples as a therapeutic chewing device. It has a hollow centre allowing treats to be inserted to give longer lasting interest. The toy bounces at irregular angles for exercise purposes. Can be left with most dogs because it is very durable and designed for the purpose.

Problems - if food is left inside it can go off.

Nylon Chews - Strong nylon chew toys manufactured in various styles and weights. Most are designed to be left with the dog for chewing, some are good for plaque control.

Problems - some become stippled or snagged and this encourages the build up of fluff and hairs which can be difficult to get off.

Whistles

Whistles come in a variety of designs and are intended for a variety of uses. It is a good idea to teach all dog owners how to use a general whistle, and incorporate this with teaching the recall, as this is invaluable when the dog is at a distance and the wind is against the power of the handler's voice.

Gundog Whistles - These come in plastic and have a variety of pitches. They are reference numbered so that the dog owner can replace them with exactly the same pitch. They are an ideal general purpose whistle as there is nothing to go wrong and they are simple to use. There is also a horn version which of course cannot be reproduced exactly, but still makes a very useful whistle that looks attractive.

Silent Whistle (pitch variable) - This is the traditional training whistle, but the variable edition is often too complicated for the average pet owner who spends time fiddling about with the variations in pitch. The whistle is of course not silent, just very high pitched, and perhaps overrated as a dog training whistle.

Sheepdog Whistle - Sometimes called the 'bent penny' because originally this is what they were made from. This is the traditional whistle of the professional shepherd. It is also known as the 'palate whistle', because it fits into the mouth. To get a range of sounds the dog trainer uses their tongue to direct air through a hole in the whistle. This takes a lot of practice to perfect. Trainers should learn to whistle a tune on the sheepdog whistle before attempting to use it for training the dog.

The whistles are made from a variety of materials, most commonly plastic, aluminium and stainless steel.

Other Whistles - There are of course many types of whistle, any of which could be used to train a dog but, perhaps care should be taken if using a whistle normally used in a sporting situation, the handler may find their dog recalling to the referee!

Other Devices and Gadgets

There are many gadgets and devices available to the unsuspecting dog owning public, some of course will have real benefit if used correctly, while others are less useful or even counter productive. In this section I have chosen a few of the more common ones, no doubt by the time that this book is published there will be many more.

My advice with these, and any other training equipment, is that you try out and fully evaluate any item, before trying to teach others to use it.

Stop Alarm - Originally designed for personal security but introduced to dog training in the UK by Dr Roger Mugford. The alarm emits a loud screech sound and can be used to stop attacks, aggression, barking etc. Can be effective as part of a training programme.

Training Discs - Designed by the late John Fisher training discs are similar to the original use of keys or other noise stimulus e.g. pebbles in a tin can, to stop a dog doing something undesirable and to teach alternative behaviour. Effective if used as part of a training programme.

Clickers - Introduced by dolphin trainer Karen Pryor from the USA. The animal is taught that when he hears the sound of the clicker, food is coming. Behaviours are shaped to desired level. Clickers are effective if introduced and used correctly.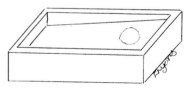

Dazzer - The Dazzer emits a high frequency sound when activated by handler. It is used to surprise or stop attack.

Bite Back - Aerosol that gives off harmless, non toxic spray with high peppermint smell that deters dogs that are aggressive sufficiently to take control of the situation.

Detonator - Sold in joke shops, gives off loud bang when disturbed. Used to stop dogs touching things. There are possible dangers if misused or when used with sensitive dogs.

Canine Development & Learning

The dog, like all animals, goes through a progression of stages of development which affect him both physically and mentally, these are often referred to as 'critical stages'. Many things can affect these stages including genetics, environment, level of care, nutrition, stress and so on. Each stage can be clearly seen in dogs by the way they behave. There are obvious physical changes in some stages that help identify the progression taking place, but more often it is the marked changes in behaviour and emotional reactions that will alert the instructor as to what stage in his development the dog has reached. Although you may not see the dog in the early stages of development, an understanding of what happens and how it affects future development is of paramount importance.

Prenatal Stage, Conception - birth

The uterine environment can have an effect on the puppies ultimate behaviour. Research in this area has been largely done on rats and humans, but from this information we can assume that dogs are not any different in that nutrition, stress, and activity levels can all have an effect on the unborn pup, therefore it is important that breeders keep the breeding bitch in excellent all round condition. Pregnant bitches should not come into contact with or consume chemicals including unnecessary drugs, or suffer from infestations of parasites or disease.

Neonatal Stage, 0 - 2 weeks

During this period there is almost no electroencephalogram activity - (electrical fluctuations in the brain - brain waves). The brain of the pup is soft and jelly like (barely myelinated) and is still developing.

The pup will tend to spend around 90% of its time in a deep sleep. He will be sensitive to touch, pain, temperature, scent and taste. However, the touch and pain sensation is slow because pups are born with touch reflexes in the head only. His hearing, sight and temperature regulation are very underdeveloped and therefore of little use to him. He is susceptible to stress.

He will develop a pup mother bond during this time, he will become imprinted to his mother and she to him, and will be dependent on her for all his needs. In the earliest stages she will even have to nuzzle and push him towards her teats in order for him to suckle, but once there he is able to follow the scent of the mother's saliva to find a teat. How his mother treats him and even her own general behavioural tendencies will have a marked effect on the rest of his life.

This is the most common time for pups to die due to abnormalities or stresses, or for breeders to cull any malformed individuals.

Dr Michael Fox did tests on pups and found that regular handling (which in effect is a mild stress), during this period will make for more well adjusted domestic animals who mature faster, make fewer mistakes when problem solving and 'kept their cool' better than pups who are not handled. However too much stress will lead to the pup developing more slowly and perhaps never reaching his true potential.

Transitional Stage, 2 - 4 weeks

The period is called the transitional period because it marks the time when the pup is transforming from a defenceless and vulnerable newly born into a reactionary, lively and aware young animal, brought about by his sensory abilities coming on line.

Eye lids open, ears open, teeth appear, tail wagging starts, the brain becomes stimulated by sights and sounds, he learns to growl and bark, he is able to regulate his own temperature, his pain response is similar to an adult, he chooses to suckle, he stimulates regurgitation in the bitch, he learns to beg, weaning begins, mother/young conflict starts and his reflexes develop. Around two weeks of age the touch reflexes have reached the front legs and the pup will be able to sit and at around three weeks they will have progressed to the hind legs allowing him to stand, then within a few days he will be co-ordinated enough to walk.

By the fourth week the brain is almost fully myelinated and he is now ready for complex learning. His sleep pattern changes and now includes light sleep before he goes into the deep sleep of dreams.

The mother's influence is still strong, but around the fourth week, conflict will start. This is driven by the fact that the mother's 'fight/flight' instinct has been subdued during the early weeks, but now as weaning starts it comes back.

Towards the end of this period the pup enters the most important 8 weeks of his life! What he experiences now will affect him for the rest of his life. Evolution has determined that it is in the dogs' interest to respond to the things that the mother introduces him to, and to learn from her example what is safe and what is not. Beyond these 8 weeks the time will come that he ventures out alone. Therefore it is in his interests to be naturally wary of anything he has not seen before, or that he is unsure of, in case it is a predator.

Socialisation Stage - 4 - 6 weeks to dogs
4 - 12 weeks to humans and other animals

Now we are into the most important time of the pup's life. His senses are now much more mature and his brain had developed sufficiently to allow him to process information quickly and very well considering the pup's limited experiences.

Play helps to develop the pup's mind, it becomes an important part of his life starting at 3 - 4 weeks. He will learn the play bow that invites his litter mates to join in his game and he learns through play to become a hunter. He learns co-ordination, safe exploration, physical and mental dexterity, chasing, ambushing, running, action patterns, sequences, timing - when to intercept/intervene. He also learns through this play how much pain to inflict when he bites, i.e. how to inhibit his bite, keeping his mouth soft, to encourage continued play with his litter mates and others. Play helps to develop bonds and stimulates communal behaviour. It moulds the pup ready for adult social behaviour. By observing the litter you may be able to detect those who will ultimately have a tendency to be dominant and those who will be more likely to be submissive, although it is only towards the end of this period that the true picture starts to emerge and of course so much can change because of circumstances.

Pups will carry small objects and play tug of war with litter mates. They will defend food and objects (quite vigorously in some breeds). Several pups will follow one who has an object, this gives us the first signs of the pups working together in a pack.

He explores the pecking order and finds his place. The bitch's severity can have a life long effect on his behaviour. For instance, the pup can become extremely submissive because of a severe mother and having experienced this, a female pup can go on to become a severe mother herself. Pups who have had no dominance from their mother usually end up very difficult to train because they have a tendency to be out of control, whereas those who have had a very severe mother may end up far to submissive to train. Obviously the best dogs come from mothers who apply just enough dominance. However, it is not a simple matter of dominance and submission there are so many other factors that will effect future behaviour.

Bad experiences or isolation can lead to the pup becoming hyper-aggressive, introverted, withdrawn, inhibited, display poor maternal behaviour, self mutilate, have a fear of people, other animals, noises, be reluctant to explore or become excessively excitable. Dogs that don't meet people until after the socialisation period will be fearful and anti-social and very difficult to train. It they have not met other dogs they are not able to interact well with others and will make poor mothers. If not dogs but plenty of people they will be very human oriented and may train quite easily except when in the company of other dogs. These type are often the ones who see humans as sex objects too!

Facial expressions are developed at around 5 weeks because the ears become more mobile, the muzzle elongates and the muscles that control the lips are improved.

This is the optimum time for pups to be socialised with other dogs, people, other animals, new environments and so on.

The best time to leave the litter and go to a new home is 7 weeks, thus allowing time to reap the benefits of being in a litter and time to learn about their new life - while still in this important critical period.

First Fear Response Stage, 5 - 12 weeks

During the socialisation period the pup enters the first fear impact stage, so care must be taken that he is introduced to new things in a very positive and supportive way. When he is in the first stages his recovery is usually quite quick but later it takes longer. Any traumatic event during this period will have a lasting effect on his life, in fact more than if the same event had occurred at any other time of his life.

Seniority Classification Stage, 12 - 16 weeks

The pup is turning into an adult, his confidence will grow and he starts to test out who is boss. This period is also known as the age of cutting both the mother's apron strings and teeth! Although we still see the dog as a pup, we should not allow him to take liberties that we would not allow from a fully grown dog otherwise his behaviour will later become a problem.

Flight Instinct Stage, 16 weeks - 8 months

At this stage the dog has a tendency to go off on his own. He turns a deaf ear to his owner. This can last a few days or a few weeks. Careful control is needed at this stage to avoid problems. Dogs who are controlled and not allowed to enter into this behaviour during this stage are far less likely to be difficult in the future. Dogs can be given freedom, but in a controlled environment and without the owner having the need to call them back.

Juvenile & Onset of Puberty, 5 months-14 months

During this period there is a gradual improvement in skills, strength and activity. The young dog will learn the relevance of his behaviours and although his attention span and motor skills will be poor he will have a fully developed learning capacity. As early as four months of age he may start to hunt.

Most of what happens during this period will be determined by what took place during the socialisation period, but the dog will need continued socialisation to make sure he can be guided into becoming well adjusted and appropriately behaved.

Males At around 18 weeks the level of testosterone starts to rise and his attitude will start to change. Dogs learn to lift their leg and this is one of the first signs of puberty. They will learn to observe territorial boundaries, attempt to mount bitches and show interest in on heat bitches from four months, but they are unlikely to have the strength or skills to be successful until around 7 - 8 months of age. At around about a year a dog is sexually mature but lacks the social skills of an older dog. Social learning is an on going process throughout the dog's life.

Females For bitches the dividing line from juvenile to adulthood can be an overnight process which usually coincides with the onset of the first heat. Males find her attractive and she shows increasing interest in them.

Adolescence and Second Fear Response Stage, 5/6 months - 11/14 months

During adolescence the dog will go through another fear period similar to the one during his socialisation period. This is because of the hormonal changes going on in his still developing body. It is very much akin to the changes in the human. The dog has adult desires and behaviours but lacks the social skills and experience to utilise them correctly. He will sometimes be fearful of things that he was not previously fearful of. He will often be afraid to approach something new. Of course his response to these fears may now be more powerful, if often comes as a shock to owners when their previously well behaved dog gives an aggressive outburst towards something or someone the dog previously accepted. How these fears are handled will have a lasting effect on his future behaviour.

Maturity/Adulthood,
(Second seniority period at onset) 1 - 4 years

In many breeds the bitches will become more mature and display adult behaviours sooner than the males, this is more marked in the larger breeds. Maturity is marked by a testing of leadership of the pack or 'Second seniority period'.

Guidance is needed throughout this period and indeed throughout the animal's life if to maintain control. It is easy to assume that a fully grown animal has well developed mental powers, of course like humans social and accepted learning is on going and the results are dependent on circumstance which can of course change.

Selective breeding has made maturity quite early but, full social maturity in the majority of breeds comes at the time that coincides with the puberty of wolves, around 2 years.

Canine Learning

There are many things that will influence canine learning, genetics, health, age, past experience, hormones, motivation, distractions and of course the way in which things are taught.

The dog, like humans needs to be taught in a way that he can under-stand. It should be remembered that he does not speak the human language, he cannot understand concepts, and does not possess the power of lateral thinking. Often the poor dog is credited with far more 'intelligence' than he is capable of. This is unfair to the animal because ultimately he will be deemed to have let his owner down, when really he just did not fully understand.

His mind can be compared to a computer. The computer comes to us ready programmed to react to certain things but, in order to react in a way that we desire, the computer must be 'programmed' to comply. Further more, we must put this information over to the computer in a language that it understands, there is no point in pleading with it, swearing at it, or even hitting it, it will only comply if it understands!

The dog is very similar, for instance the word 'Sit' means nothing to him until we show him what is required when we say that word. This has to be done in a way he can understand, and he must be motivated suffi-ciently to make him want to comply. Then following some successful repetitions, in a variety of environments and circumstances, we may have the desired result.

The dog's memory is different to ours in that he cannot choose to think backwards and forwards at will. His memory needs to be triggered by certain circumstances, sounds, actions, sights, smells, tastes, feels etc.

Dogs react to triggers, i.e. what confronts the dog he will react to, that reaction will be dependent on previous experience, motivation, distractions, homeostasis and so on. All senses trigger reactions as do hormones so, training a dog effectively is far more complex than we might at first think. The dog is able to carry out complex tasks because each 'trigger' acts as a catalyst to activate the next action.

Many of his actions are based on his drive to survive. His desire to play is closely related to his need for food, because play is the way that he learns to hunt.

Dogs learn through a variety of mediums, including classical conditioning, observation, extinction, flooding, habituation, systematic desensitisation, reinforcement, operant conditioning, chaining. (*See definitions*). One of the best ways for complex learning is to put the dog in a pleasant environment, provide him with a motivation, and then allow or guide him into working things out for himself.

Training of anything that has more than one component should be chained, teach the dog one small segment and then link it with another. Wherever possible start at the end and work back. With positive reinforcement the dog will be well motivated and the tasks themselves will become self motivating.

Problem Behaviours

In this section we look at problem behaviours most likely to manifest themselves in the home. Jumping up and barging through doorways, could also be classed as problem behaviours but are covered in the techniques section because they are likely to happen in class. Common for almost all handlers they really should be covered in practical sessions.

A good and dedicated dog training instructor can deal with almost all problem behaviours, but is should be noted that some behaviours may need one to one tuition due to the complex nature or potential dangers of the problem.

It is advisable for instructors just starting out, or unacquainted with some of these problems to refer them to a behaviour specialist until competence is guaranteed. Of course you cannot learn without being involved, so keep learning and try to sit in on some of the more complex problems that you refer to others.

Counter Conditioning (Distraction Training)

One of the most common and effective means of re-focusing a dog is to counter condition (sometimes termed distraction training). This means to teach the dog to focus onto something else, instead of what it is that causes him to behave in an inappropriate manner. For problem areas like chasing, interaction problems and so on, where the owner fights a loosing battle every time they come into that situation, teaching a new and powerful behaviour will give them the control and confidence they need.

Powerful is the operative word. The behaviour needs to be powerful, i.e. the dog needs to want to do it at least as much, preferably more, than he wants to do things that are inappropriate.

The handler should be advised to find a toy or a reward that the dog will 'sell his soul' for. A squeaky toy is great because it is audible, but it is more important that the dog likes it.

Next the handler needs to take other toys out of the way so that the

155

dog cannot look elsewhere for his fun. At the same time the handler needs to work on mentally, and often physically distancing him or herself from the dog so that the dog is craving their attention instead of getting it on demand.

Once this has been achieved the handler should start to play with the toy - if the dog offers to join in he should be allowed - if not he should be ignored and the handler should make an issue of having some fun, all the while ignoring the dog. A short session of this and then the toy is put away.

The next day the session is repeated, and so on. Soon the dog will start to be more keen to join in. The handler should always be the one to finish the game, and to maintain control of the dog and the toy. The game should be finished leaving the dog wanting more.

It is good idea now to give the game a name or a sound cue, so that the dog can easily be turned onto the fun both by using his eyes and his ears, and probably his nose too.

It is a good idea, while all of this training is going on, to try to avoid any of the problem situations if at all possible, because every time the problem arises, the handler is in effect condoning it, no matter what their reaction is.

The handler should reach the stage, with careful planning and control, that the dog will turn to have a game anytime the handler gives the key. It is important to train the game in a variety of situations.

Once the handler has grown confident of this, the dog can be taken to a mildly distracting place and the same game instigated. It should be remembered that the dog will easily lapse back into his old behaviour if the handler allows the situation to occur. The handler must act before the situation becomes a problem and guide the dog away to have some fun.

Dominance

One of the most common problems that the instructor will have to recognise and give advice on is dominance.

Often the problem goes undetected for sometime as many owners dismiss little challenges as part of the dog growing up. A grumble over food, or maybe a growl over being moved or worse still the dog bites, or attempts to, in a similar situation. The warning signs are there and need to be identified before things get out of hand. Often, dog owners will allow, or live with, certain behaviours in the guise of having 'a quiet life'. In class you can ask direct questions that will help you to gauge if a problem is brewing.

Some breeds of dog have more dominant types than others. A good instructor will not jump to conclusions but, whenever faced with the following breeds, particular attention should be taken: Doberman, Rottweiler, Cocker Spaniel, Lhasa Apso, German Shepherd, Bull Breeds and Terriers. Generally any breed that has been bred to be in control of certain situations.

That is not to say that other breeds are immune. Any dog can be born with dominant tendencies or learn to become dominant. Some owners have the uncanny knack of making the most submissive of dogs into a dominant character. Normally inherent dominance is more prevalent in males.

Recognising Dominance

Asking questions about where the dog sleeps, if it ever growls or shows a dominant body stance and in what circumstances, will reveal if dogs are showing dominant tendencies, the amount of inadvertent, dominance building occurrences can be endless.

Some dogs can be allowed 'privileges', and never be a problem to their owners, because the dog is not generally of a dominant nature or because other situations tip the balance and the dog accepts his place. But, given enough of the correct dominance building situations, most dogs can become dominant to one degree or another, even if the dominance only shows or is a problem in certain situations (circumstantial dominance).

There are two distinct types of dominance - social and possessive. Socially dominant dogs take the lead role in the pack were as possessive dominant dogs only take charge of food, objects, space or sometimes people. Some dogs may only be one type or the other, while others fall into both categories.

Learning to recognise the dominant stance is important. The dog will stand upright, square and erect, his ears forward and tail held high. Obviously some breeds naturally stand like this, but if you observe closely you will see the difference between the passive stance and the dominant one. However, in cases of possessive dominance the dog may maintain a lower posture, but give other signals such as showing of teeth, snarling or snapping.

Controlling Dominance

The owner will need advice on how to build up a pattern of behaviour in the dog that informs his instincts that he is no longer in control and taking the dominant role. This is done by the way in which they live their lives. Following are a set of rules to give to owners that will help them control and prevent dominant behaviour.

Rule One - Do **not** lay on the floor nor allow the dog to freely lay on you. Take the dominant role by remaining above the dog both physically and mentally. If you do allow the dog to be on top of you, a dog with dominant tendencies will feel very much in control of you.

Rule Two - Collect all the dog's toys and keep them out of his reach in a drawer or cupboard. These must now remain in **your** possession. Don't feel that you are being mean or depriving the dog because you will be making up for this amply with your attention to training and control. The dog's life will soon become much more fulfilled than it ever was before, because in order to control him, and keep him under control you will have to work hard.

Rule Three - Games must be instigated by **you** not the dog. Only play when **you** want to, when you feel in control, and when the dog is obviously under the impression that **you** started the game. The dog must not be allowed to think that he started the game even if **you** feel that he did not, do not cheat on yourself. **You** must always be the one to finish with the prize.

Rule Four - Do not throw toys and allow the dog to run off and take possession of them, play should be enjoyed with the dog on lead under your complete control. If the dog should win by accident, bring him back to you by finding some form of reward that he would like even more than the toy that he has in his possession, a different toy or titbit for instance. Always have something in your pocket to aid you in control. Encourage him to sit down or do some other control exercise for the reward and then you have regained control.

Rule Five - If you are playing tug games a titbit can be used in conjunction with the keyword 'Leave' to get the dog to release on command, avoid tug games until you **know** you can win.

Rule Six - Do not allow the dog to become obsessive over games that he might tend to play on his own. Discourage any repetitive stereo-typic actions by distracting him onto other things. Repetitive stereotypic behaviour is the type of behaviour that can be seen in some zoo animals, repetitive seemingly meaningless actions often heightened by boredom, excitement and frustration. Animals need plenty of stimulating activities and varying environments to prevent this behaviour. Allowing this behaviour to carry on with a dominant dog often results in aggression when his drive is interrupted.

Rule Seven - Do not stare at the dog eye to eye. If he has this tendency, make a mental note to look to the side, turning your head to turn off his power and calm him. Distract him with a toy, then ignore him, act naturally and do not instigate a stare out if it can be avoided.

Rule Eight - Do not allow him to demand attention for any reason, even if it is to attend to his bodily functions such as food or toilet. Anticipate his needs and organise events so that you can make him do something else, or so that he is busy doing something else when **YOU** tell him that it is time for toilet, food etc.

Rule Nine - Do not position his bed in an area that he can easily guard such as a cosy corner of a room. If he is displaying guarding or dominance tendencies over his bed, call him out of the room before you move the bed, this will help avoid confrontation. Move it on a regular basis, make sure that he will allow you to go freely into his bed area and do this several times a day at least.

Rule Ten - Do not allow him free access to **your** bed area, to the entrance to your bedroom, or even to the hall or landing leading to your bed. Top dogs have an exclusive bed area, make sure yours is exclusive to you, and the dog's bed area should be readily available to all the family.

Rule Eleven - Do not allow the dog to barge through doorways ahead of you. This may mean restricting access for the dog until you have trained the control exercises. Use your lead to make sure you have control of the dog, make him sit and then you go through the doorway first. Top dogs inspect the surroundings first, make sure **YOU** are top dog.

Rule Twelve - Top dogs make it obvious to their pack that they have the option of eating first. Feed your dog after you and your family have eaten. If this is not always possible, make sure the dog sees you eating something while you are preparing his meal, even if you have to pretend to eat his food! If the situation is such that the dog has been fed before the family, put him out of the way, in another room or outside, so that he does not watch you eat while he sits there with a full stomach.

Rule Thirteen - Do not allow the dog to eat in a corner of a room. You may need to change the room in which you feed him if already his food dominance is getting out of hand, (i.e. he is growling or snarling over food), thus giving you fresh ground and the leading stance.

Rule Fourteen - Teach the dog that you are in control of food by following this simple training procedure:

Prepare the food in a bowl. Offer a morsel of food on a small dish separately, keeping control of the main dish. When the first offering is eaten with no growling or aggression offer another piece. Continue this process until all of the meal is eaten. Bringing the dish back and replenishing it, will teach the dog that you are more likely to give more food than to take the food away. If there is any sign of growling or aggression, withdraw and offer no more food. Try again later. You may find better control if you change the room where you feed and you put the dog under the control of his lead. The dog will soon learn that you are in control of the food and that you offer more food when he responds correctly.

Once you are confident, allow the dog a little more food at a time and alternate this with putting the dish on the floor. Keep up this procedure of control at each meal until you and each member of the family, including children, are completely confident. It is important that the dog sees all the family in the same light, (i.e. above him in the hierarchy), but do not put your children at risk of being bitten, be sure that you are in complete control of the dog first, and control your children in this exercise. Make sure the dog is aware that you are backing the children. Instruct the child allowing him to watch you first and then stand immediately behind to guide and give confidence. Do not get cross with the child, as the dog may think it is his duty to help you (the top dog) to chastise the underling (child)!

Rule Fifteen - Train your dog at home using the techniques shown in class, and make sure that you are able to maintain full control at all times. Continue training the dog on a regular basis, even after you believe the dog understands what is required. Repeating the training procedures will help you to maintain complete control of your dog.

Some Do's & Don'ts For Keeping Good Control

Do not be afraid of putting the dog on a lead, even in the house, when situations are likely to be at their most difficult or when added control is needed.

This may be especially important at the start of training, when visitors are expected or any other time that the handler needs complete control or extra confidence. Having a treat available to use as a reward for the dog's good behaviour and to encourage good conduct will help to promote good results in the future.

Do not threaten the dog into the control exercises, he should be firmly controlled, and yet taught in a friendly, non-aggressive manner.

Do not avoid situations that the dog does not like, or where he has shown signs of dominance or aggression, although you must prevent putting yourself in a situation where you risk being bitten. Alter the circumstances so that you can take control and feel confident in handling the situation. Start at a distance where appropriate and work back to problem areas slowly building up your own confidence.

Do not be too predictable or over repetitive in your daily routine or training programme. An intelligent dog will soon start trying to take the lead role, anticipating your next move if you do so.

Do teach your dog to accept and enjoy being groomed. If he does not like it, distract him with a toy or titbit and start very gently bit by bit each day with a soft brush, building up the volume of the area that you cover until you can touch the whole of your dog's body. Grooming is a very natural part of a dog's social behaviour he must learn to readily accept being groomed by you.

Do make sure that your dog has plenty of activities which involve your control training sessions, games started by you, changes of environment, excursions to new places etc. This will stimulate his mind to accept your control and use up excess energy.

Do stick to the rules if you want to maintain control of your dominant or potentially dominant dog.

Separation Problems

Two of the major problem areas that cause dog owners to contact behavioural consultants or dog trainers to help sort out their problems are; (1) chewing or destructive behaviour and (2) howling or barking when the owner is out. These problems are also one of the common reasons for dogs being sent to rescue centres, because the owners just cannot cope with the problems any more. They may have suffered complaints from neighbours, or worse had official notices served on them, because of the noise their dog makes when he is left alone.

The dog is a pack animal and it is a great wrench to be alone. In fact it is very cruel to leave him for long periods without first introducing a suitable training programme that will give him confidence.

Activity and Stimulation

In many cases the problem will be connected to lack of exercise and/or stimulation. Few owners realise how much the average active dog needs.

Quality exercise is needed. A straining walk around the block on a lead is more likely to stress the dog than make him feel better. He needs free running exercise, this can be on an extending line or washing line if recalls are a problem.

He needs mental stimulation, tossing a ball is okay to begin with, but teaching a variety of tricks and activities will be much better. A walk in an interesting environment such as a wood, long grass, beach, lake side, even a busy market place will provide more stimulation than an open playing field. The inventive owner will use the environment around them, encouraging the dog to jump small barriers and open spaces, weave around things, even climb on things. If the exercise area lacks interest the owner could create their own by hiding toys, treats etc. Alternatively more structured searching or Sendaway games could be set up.

Of course advice must be given on the individual dog's needs. If the dog is unfit, still growing, heavy boned, nervous or aggressive etc., there may be special issues that need to be explained.

Training Programme
To Prevent or Treat Separation Anxiety

An area of the home needs to be selected that is safe for the dog to start his training. Avoid areas where the dog will see the owner going out, as this will heighten his anxiety level. Ideally select an area where the dog can be left to his own devices and cannot do much damage, (to property or to himself), and if his bladder lets him down, (or worse), the area can be easily cleaned and no one will be annoyed.

Dogs like a cosy corner or an area that feels secure. Crates are a great idea, and could perhaps be sold through your class. They have the added benefits of helping the dog to be clean. He will not want to foul his own bed area, and if restricted to his crate he will be more inclined to hold himself until released. Crates also prevent the dog running around and getting himself excited, they prevent him from having access to start to chewing the wrong things. If the owner does decide to use a crate then advice on how to get him used to it needs to be given, using food rewards to build up good associations in a similar way as below.

Once the area where the dog is to be left has been decided the next step is to place the dog's bed, blanket or crate there. A keyword needs to be chosen that in the future will mean to the dog, 'go to this area', for instance 'Bed', or 'Crate', or 'Blanket'.

The dog is encouraged into the area using a chew or treat or simply by taking him there on lead. The dog is put into a down position and given a chew treat. The treat should preferably one that will last the dog a while. The handler stays with the dog until he has finished the treat. The dog is then called away from the area, and whole procedure is started again a little later. It can be repeated several times to build up a good association with this place.

The handler should be encouraged to stay relatively aloof from the dog - the reward should come more from the place rather than the handler. A good time to train is when the dog is tired, he can be encouraged to lie down and perhaps sleep. The handler should sit on a chair near him and read a book, (preferably on dog training!)

If the dog pesters the handler he or she should ignore him, eventually the dog will lay down and go to sleep. The handler should leave the dog to sleep for a while, and then wake him and give a small reward.

Then the handler should go about their business, staying in the vicinity of the dog, but ignoring him to lessen the dog/owner dependency. A game can be started by the owner once the dog is detached, but the owner should maintain control by finishing the game too.

The whole procedure can be repeated often until the dog starts to become accustomed to the exercise.

Once he is happily on his bed chewing his treat and the handler has stayed in the same room with him, another treat or chew toy can be given just prior to the owner going out of the room for a moment. The owner should come straight back and reward the dog.

The next step is to go out, close the door, come back, reward. This is repeated several times.

If the dog should start to become distressed the progression is too fast.

Little by little the time that the dog is alone is lengthened, with the handler being just in the next room.

It is important that this training session is set up. Advise the handler not to wait until they have to leave the dog to test the training.

It is a good idea to leave the house as normal as possible. A radio or the television can be left on for the dog, this helps to blank out any external noises that might worry him and also helps to disguise the void that the handler has left behind. In some cases it is even beneficial to leave a tape recording of the household or of the owner talking.

Advice should be given about the length of time a dog can be realistically left alone in the house without problems occurring. Adequate allowances must be made for his needs. To expect an adult dog to last more than four hours alone in a house is not fair to the animal. To expect a puppy to last this long is even less fair. A couple of hours for a pup, once he has gone through his training and is happy to be left, is quite sufficient. If the owner has to leave the dog longer on a regular basis, then advice on getting an outside enclosure, or possibly even a companion should be given although, of course, both these solutions can bring their own problems. The welfare of the animal should come first.

Chewing

Chewing can be related to separation anxiety or can purely be a problem on its own. Anxious dogs will chew, therefore they need to be treated as above as well as the following.

Chewing is quite simply a natural dog behaviour. It helps to keep teeth in good condition, it helps new teeth to come through and in the wild the dog, or rather its ancestor the wolf, would regularly spend time chewing on bones, bits of wood etc. Therefore, it is a good idea to provide suitable chew items for the dog to direct and exercise this natural behaviour.

Choosing the right sort of chew toy can be a bonus when the dog is to be left for longer periods. The toy should be safe and most importantly, designed to be a chew. Hollow chew toys can be stuffed with treats, bits of meat, cheese, biscuits or a mixture of the dog's favourite foods. This can keep the dog occupied for hours, until he eventually falls asleep.

Chew toys should not be left scattered around for the dog when the owner is at home. They should be saved for when the dog is to be left alone and picked up and cleaned out when the owner returns. This way they are always fresh to the dog, and he is far less likely to become bored with them and look for other things to chew.

Roasted, sterilised, smoked and marrowbones are good alternatives but do carry some risks.

Barking and Howling - Noise Pollution

In some countries the laws regarding noise pollution are very strict resulting in some dogs being de-barked. This is not a very pleasant solution, usually the more acceptable remedy lies in better management of the animal.

Barking is a normal natural behaviour for dogs, they seldom bark at nothing. Dogs usually have a reason, even though at first the reason may be difficult to detect. For example, their hearing is different to ours and therefore they pick up sounds that we do not.

Dogs in isolation make a noise in a natural response to what their senses tell them. Therefore they may well bark or whine when they see movement or hear a noise. This movement or noise can be common things such as traffic, children other dogs or animals, but may also be less common e.g. the noise of sudden bangs, vehicles back firing, fireworks, thunder etc., or the sudden movement of something falling, an intruder and so on. They may feel excitement, endure the loneliness of solitary confinement, changes in air pressure, wind or weather. They may smell the scent of food, other dogs or animals. Indeed there are many factors that may encourage noise from the dog.

Therefore it is best to look at barking in differing categories: alarm, greeting, threat, territorial, play and social.

Each noise case needs to be dealt with individually as every one's circumstances are different - but there are some guidelines that can be followed along with a retraining programme:

Barking during owner absence

1 Is the dog suffering from separation anxiety? If so treat as above.
2 If the dog barks at the phone or door bell these can be turned off during owner absences.
3 If the dog is excited by external noises curtains can be closed, radio or TV left on. The dog can be left in a room or area where stimuli are less likely to trigger the behaviour.
4 It may be that the dog barks at certain things. Neighbours will perhaps help to make this diagnosis. Once the cause is identified the solution may be to take away or prevent interaction with that stimuli.*
5 It could be that the confinement is the cause of the problem in that it is unacceptable in duration. Dogs who are left alone for long periods become hypersensitive to noise and other stimuli because there is nothing else for them to do. The answer is leave for less time, or provide a more suitable environment and stimulus for the dog.
6 During retraining it will be necessary to find some way of preventing the behaviour. Not leaving the dog alone or employing a dog sitter may be the only (or short term) answer.
7 Make sure the dog has adequate opportunities to let off steam, before confinement, i.e. good quality walks with free play, games and training mixed in with lead walking. Ten minutes around the block is not enough for any dog.

*For all these the dog can also be counter conditioned with a training programme. (*See counter conditioning*).

During Owner Presence

It is surprising how many dogs are noisy during owner presence.

Again the causes are many and, if the reasons are as above then the remedy will be the same or similar.

If both dog and owner are confined for some reason then exercise and stimulating activities can be achieved in the house. Training sessions and play activities do not have to be outside.

Owners often reinforce barking by giving in to the attention or demand bark. Owners must learn to ignore the bark or put it under stimulus control. It is often easiest to teach the dog to bark on command in order to control the bark.

Most owners want their dog to bark if an intruder is identified, therefore to stop the dog barking entirely is unrealistic as well as unnatural.

To get the bark on command owners can use a stimuli to which the dog already barks. The doorbell is a common one. The session is set up with someone helping the owner. The doorbell is rung by the helper and the handler gives their keyword for bark, perhaps the word 'Speak', just prior to the bell being rung. The dog will soon learn that when it hears the word 'Speak' the bell will follow and he will start to anticipate the bell and bark when the handler says 'Speak'. The dog is verbally rewarded.

The training session should be extended to include 'Quiet'. As the barking dies down, turn the dog's attention away from the stimuli, introduce the keyword 'Quiet', and then, when the dog has been quiet for a couple of seconds, reward the dog verbally or with a treat.

Most owners who's dogs bark too much will be obsessed by the noise and forget that there are times when the dog is quiet, and therefore good. They should be reminded that these times should be used to reward and play with the dog so that he learns that he gets good quality attention when he is quiet.

There are times when it is acceptable to bark - perhaps when out for a walk in an isolated area - it is okay then to allow and indeed encourage the dog to have a good bark and perhaps get some of it out of his system.

Barking In Class

Dealing with barkers or whiners in class is always a difficult area. If the handlers had the ability to quieten the dog they would no doubt do it, so it is pointless merely asking them to keep the dog quiet as I have observed with some trainers.

Owners need to be taught to observe and react to the warning signs, i.e. the signs that the dog gives off just prior to the barking. It may be instigated by eye to eye contact with other dogs, it may be when there is movement on the floor, it may be to certain dogs or people it barks at, it may also be due to sheer frustration or excitement.

Therefore, first assess the situation and, if necessary, move the handler and dog to an area where the handler will be able to gain better control.

In most cases the dog needs to be given an alternative behaviour to keep him occupied, play or some other reward based exercise is a good alternative.

Most handlers with barking dogs will not be armed with play toys or treats, therefore you will have to assess the dog and decide what to use for the best, perhaps giving both a try or using a combination. Show the handler how to play interactively with their dog, then keep an eye on them until they become accustomed to anticipating the barking behaviour and interrupting the flow with a game or a reward - before the dog starts. It is important that they realise that they must anticipate and not react afterwards, otherwise the dog may feel he is being rewarding for barking. The handler will need reassurance that his games with the dog are not disturbing the class.

Aversion therapy can work. Some trainers use water pistols squirted at the dog to stop it from barking. This painless, although wet experience can work quickly for some dogs, but could instil fear which may be misdirected. Dogs should not be repeatedly squirted - if it didn't work first or second time it is unlikely to work at all. Some dogs like it and try to catch the spray, it may even be counter productive resulting in a dog barking at the instructor to start that fun water game again!

Chasing

Chasing can be a real problem to owners, and is especially common in herding breeds, although none are immune. Dogs chase for two main reasons; because its fun (this is based on their drive for catching prey) and because they are chasing something away from themselves, their territory or their possessions.

If the dog chases for fun, the owner needs to be aware of how to control the urge to chase, by providing controlled chasing games with toys, if necessary, on a long line to be extra safe, or at least until the owner is sure of the dog's behaviour - (*see counter conditioning*).

If the dog is chasing because he is chasing something away the major cause of this is fear, (fear of the thing he is chasing or fearful of loss of position or possession etc.) Therefore a programme needs to be set up to teach the dog that what he is chasing is not something to be feared. (*See below - Fears and Phobias and Fear Aggression and above - Counter Conditioning*).

Interaction Problems

Most dogs are difficult with others because they are fearful, want to show their position or they just do not know how to react. Many are worse on lead than off, often because of the way the owner has handled the situation in the past, or because the dog feels trapped by the restriction. Some dogs are just so social that they are desperate to get to the other dog to have some fun.

In class you may be able to help by allowing controlled interaction, but you must be sure of the dogs temperaments. A sound well socialised and adjusted dog can teach an uncertain dog a lot about how to react in just a few sessions.

The easiest way of dealing with other problems is to use distraction training (counter conditioning) to get the dog focused onto something else instead of the problem. (*See Counter Conditioning above*).

Often dogs who lack the skills of interaction are generally lacking in socialisation. Exercises set up such as weaving in and out will help, but it may be necessary for the dog to be allowed to stay still and watch to start with, and then gradually integrated with the class.

Flooding with lots of interaction can help too. In other words the handler needs to get to lots of places were there are a lot of dogs and people under control.

Of course the safety of all involved must be at the top of your list, but using the right equipment can help. Head collars or muzzles may be necessary to start with if the dog tends to be aggressive. (*See also growl classes.*)

Fears and Phobias

Fears

Fear is a difficult emotion to deal with, sometimes it appears to we humans, that it is an irrational reaction and it can indeed have many origins.

It is known that a potential to be highly reactive, which often leads to fear of the unknown, can be inherited. It is quite common in some breeds, the German shepherd being a prime example, but it can occur in almost any breed. Whole litters can be affected, it is always worth asking questions about the parents and siblings if inherited fear is suspected.

It is more common however, for a learned and inappropriate response driven by fear, to be common in dogs that have not been socialised correctly. It is generally accepted that temperament is derived from 25% breeding/genetics and 75% environment.

Well structured social training needs to be worked on from an early age, i.e. while the pup is still in the nest, and continued well into adult life. Often pups are taken to class when they are young, but by the time the important adolescent stage is reached, the owners have either had enough, or think they know enough, attendance and therefore social training stops - hence problems start.

Fear is a natural response inherited by all dogs from their ancestor the wolf. If dogs are not appropriately socialised with a large number of situations, smells, animals, humans and objects etc., they will be naturally fearful of anything that they do not understand. This is of course nature's defence mechanism, because in the wild, anything the animal is not sure of may prove to be a predator, therefore fear is one of nature's ways of protecting and perpetuating a species.

At around 8 to 11 weeks and then later at 6 to 15 months of age the pup is particularly susceptible to fear. These are periods that coincide with major developments for the dog. The first period would be when he first comes out of the safety of the litter and second coincides with adolescence. Any trauma during these periods is likely to stay with the dog for life. The really critical period is the first, but equally a dog that is not socialised and handled well during adolescence will become a real problem.

In tests done by Scott, (1958), it was shown that even pups born of parents that were well socialised with humans, would revert to their natural fearful and wild behaviour if brought up in an environment void of human contact.

Acquired fear is another facet of this behaviour, but one which can be a little easier to deal with because anything that is a acquired has been learnt and therefore can be counter conditioned to relieve the symptoms and change the dogs outlook on the problem.

Back in 1948 Miller experimented on rats showing that the rat could very quickly learn that when he was placed in a white box he would receive mild electric shocks but, he could escape this by retreating into a black box. Even when the shocks ceased to occur in the white box the rat would always retreat to the safety of the black box. The fear had been conditioned (learnt) and now escape driven by fear was a very positive response. Later Miller introduced a wheel that the rats learned, by trial and error, to turn to achieve their escape.

In the past the use of fear as a drive for learning has been used in the training of dogs. By issuing mild (sometimes harsh) physical pain or discomfort, the dog has to learn what behaviour is required to avoid the pain or discomfort, he is often 'helped' by some form of physical manipulation. The checking action in choke chain style heel work is a prime example of this. But, the work of Miller reveals that the animals ultimate aim is escape from fear or things that are painful, therefore he may well learn certain tasks, but his main aim will be to get away from his oppressor. If he is not allowed that option, he will learn how to exist in this regime, but will never reach the true potential that a more positive approach to learning can achieve.

Fight or flight are the most common responses to fear. Flight, i.e. the urge to run away is the most likely. But dogs denied the opportunity to run away may stand barking or growling, and will display some or all the following characteristic signs of fear; tail tucked between the legs, back arched, ears flat and to the side, hackles down the back raised, lips drawn back exposing teeth, raised heart rate, trembling, dilated pupils and urination. The dog may also become hyperexcited, restless and very alert. Of course they may resort to fight mode, i.e. they may bite or at the least give a show of aggression.

Phobias

Phobias are really extensions of fear, i.e. things that the dog has learnt to be frightened of, and although with no real foundation never learns to overcome, may be termed phobias.

Most humans harbour phobias, often seemingly ridiculous to others. For example I rather like spiders and allow them to live in harmony in certain areas of my home. Some people reading this may already be having a reaction to their phobia - arachniphobia - the fear of spiders.

A phobia does not always result in the flight/fight reaction. However, all of the anxiety related behaviours listed above may be displayed and the phobia often becomes worse because to the animals anxious reaction which is self perpetuating.

Other behaviours that occur because of phobias are, digging (sometimes into furniture) in an attempt to find a hiding place. Chewing furniture or carpets etc. which is sometimes an attempt to make an escape, or to induce endorphins, nature's natural pain killers which will help to relieve anxiety. Self mutilation, again this induces endorphins. Defecating and/or urinating inappropriately, fearful and phobic dogs have difficulty controlling themselves. Displacement activities, these are normal behaviours but, not always done in normal fashion, produced as a way of avoiding confrontation with situations which the dog finds less desirable.

Preventing and Treating Fears and Phobias

As is the lot of dog training instructors, it is likely that you are too late to look at prevention. Usually the owner presents themselves to you with the problem. However, you can sometimes identify a possible problem before it manifests, and therefore can save a lot of heartache for both the owner and dog.

- Avoiding buying pups from the bloodlines and individuals known, or that can be seen, to be carrying what could be classed as neurotic behaviour is the first step.
- Proper, gentle exposure to mildly frightening things during social training. If the dog never has to deal with adversity as a youngster he will definitely have difficulty later on, so he should not be 'wrapped in cotton wool'.
- Continued social training into adulthood.
- Counter conditioning can be highly successful where the behaviour is largely learnt.
- Flooding and habituation can work if the fear has not become a phobia.
- Confidence building exercise. Depending on the fear, gradual exposure, allowing the dog to approach the object of its fear and be rewarded for it. If the dog is pushed into meeting the fear head on he will panic and try to run or fight. The owner can approach the item that is bothering the dog first, to show there is nothing to worry about.
- Find ways of having a common bond between something the dog fears and something it enjoys. For instance a dog spooks at new things on a walk, a fallen tree, a hay bale in a field perhaps, the owner can approach the item and pat it, talk to it, sit on it, have a game with the dog's toy next to it, and then walk on. This shows the dog that the owner does not fear the object and yet the dog is not pushed into making contact. After a few occurrences the dog's confidence will grow.
- Allowing the dog its 'flight/fight distance'. We all need personal space and fearful animals need more than an animal who is bold.
- In some cases the dog needs to be given a retreat where he can feel safe at times of fear. For instance a covered cage to go into during a thunder storm if the dog has learnt previously that his cage is his haven. Good things happen there, he gets treats and cuddles etc. He will feel more secure at times of anxiety in his own area. However, it should be noted that there is a fine line between giving confidence and actually rewarding fearful behaviour. It is best that handlers anticipate the fear so they can start the confidence building before the dog has time to go into his fearful response.

Canine Aggression

It is rare to meet a truly aggressive dog because if a dog bites and bites hard it is normally euthanased. The majority of dogs that bite are actually friendly dogs that have been forced into a situation and feel that the only way to save themselves is to bite.

There are certain times that are more likely to cause the dog to bite and not all would be classed as aggressive in the real sense of the word and yet these instances can, in some cases, be just as distressing.

Dogs bite when playful, when over exuberant, when grabbed or restrained (especially by strangers), when frightened, when shy, when protecting food, bed area, toys, territory, owners, offspring, houses, cars etc., and of course when aggressive.

Aggression towards humans stems from an underlying fear, lack of confidence or trust in people. This is true of all captive animals.

Puppy bites - it a normal behaviour for pups to bite. If they do not bite as pups they do not learn 'bite inhibition' i.e. how hard to bite and when and when not to bite.

During early adolescence 6 - 15 months - the developing animal is unsure of how to react and, as all adolescents, becomes more reactionary because of this.

At maturity 1 - 3 years - the young adult starts to feel his feet and dominance testing is normally the root of bites at this stage.

At the onset of old age - the old dog like the old human becomes less agile and develops the aches and pains of old age - thus he becomes less tolerant.

Dominant Aggression

Dominance is both learned and inherited. The hormonal influence on the behaviour happens shortly after birth when testosterone masculinizes the brain and future behaviour. If genetically programmed in this way the dog will actively work towards the 'Alpha' role i.e. the position of 'Top Dog - number one in the pecking order' throughout his life. (*See above for detailed information on dominance.*)

Fear Aggression

Unlike dominant aggression, fear aggression, although it is a natural response, is largely learned and defensive. Because it is learned it is much easier to treat.

Fear aggression is the most common cause of dog bites, it is a natural response to aid self preservation and is the most common response of all captive animals towards humans.

Fear aggression is often induced during the socialisation period when natural curiosity is over taken by fear of the unknown. Fear aggression can be caused by a previous painful or frightening experience. It occurs in as many females as males and has no hormonal influence. Fear aggression is reinforced by learning.

There is some genetic influence, particularly in specific breeds for example the GSD who has an inherited 'high reactivity' to senses. (*See also Fears and Phobias*).

Preventing and Treating Fear Aggression

- Careful puppy selection - avoiding the pup cowering in the corner, although it may be too late for you to give this advice and many owners are drawn to the 'poor wee thing'.
- Proper socialisation helping the pup adapt to the environment.
- Exposing the dog in a non frightening way to possible frightening experiences e.g. traffic, noise, crowds, other dogs and animals, children, postmen, etc.
- Use rewards and behaviour patterns to counter condition and desensitise.
- Identify exact course or circumstances that promote the fear, then recreate in a less frightening way using play training, rewards and establishing common bonds.
- Never punish fear or fear aggression - it will get worse.
- Use situations that are less fearful for the dog to integrate with more frightening ones.

Intermale Aggression

Males of most domesticated species are prone to fighting with each other. Intermale aggression develops from the onset of puberty when there is a surge of testosterone which affects the already masculinised brain.

The aggression can be induced by the sight or scent of another male.

It is rare to find this type of aggression in females. Fights between females are usually dominance or possession conflicts. Even injecting females with testosterone does not normally induce aggression due to the neonatal influence.

Preventing and Treating Intermale Aggression

- Choose pups that do not show dominant masculine behaviours, but this is not a definite answer as puppy testing for this trait is not reliable because of the later testosterone influence.
- Early castration, although this can disrupt normal maturation.

- Surgical castration is thought to be effective in around 60% of cases. An extra 15% can be helped by the additional treatment of the female hormone progesterone. Castration works because within 24 hours of surgery the neural system in the brain no longer receives hormonal messages. Also the dog no longer gives off an odour that is offensive to other dogs.
Training and counter conditioning needs to be coupled with castration as the behaviour may have its roots in hormones, but it soon becomes a learnt response too. Perhaps the above figures could be improved with more effective training programmes given and followed through by the owners.
- Intermale aggression is often coupled with dominance and in some situations it is difficult to decide whether to treat one or the other or both, therefore both issues must be investigated to be sure of the correct diagnoses and subsequent treatment.
- Dominant aggression between dogs is treated by making the social gap between the dogs wider. If intermale aggression is coupled with this then the less dominant of the two should be castrated first. This makes the natural social distance bigger by eliminating the pheromones that provoke the behaviour.
- The only fool proof way is to buy a bitch!

Idiopathic Aggression

Often referred to as 'rage syndrome', 'red eye' or 'Jekyll and Hyde syndrome'. Aggression is referred to as idiopathic when the dog becomes aggressive for no apparent reason. When behaviour does not relate to dominance, fear, or any other readily definable cause.

It is thought to have its roots in genetics, it can sometimes be traced to a few individual carriers but research is patchy and still in progress.

Most common breeds said to be affected include Cocker Spaniel, English Bull Terrier, Rottweiler, Doberman, GSD, St Bernard and Bernese. However, it can occur in others.

Dogs affected are normally good natured and well behaved individuals but, for no apparent reason can suddenly become aggressive turning on their owners, visitors or even an object for no apparent reason and without warning. Some snap out of it quickly, others remain subdued for a while. Some owners might identify a glazed detached stage before an attack.

It is easy to jump to conclusions, diagnosing aggression as idiopathic when you cannot identify any other cause, especially for the inexperienced, but all other aggressions should be thoroughly explored, preferably seeking second opinions, before making this diagnoses, as there is no real cure for an idiopathic aggressive dog.

Of course idiopathic aggression can be coupled with other sorts of aggression as well.

Preventing and Treating Idiopathic Aggression

Sometimes there is more likelihood of a problem within specific lines and even certain colours. For instance in the case of cockers, who are perhaps the most well known for this problem, it was thought that it was more likely to occur in the reds, as this is where it was seen the most. But, this research was done at a time when reds were very popular and so it was easy for the statistics to be misinterpreted. Current research shows that all solid coloured cockers are equally likely to be affected and parti coloured less so.

Research on subjects such as this is very difficult due to some breeder ethics (or rather lack of ethics). Also, many breeders loose touch with puppy owners and problems are not reported to the breeder. Affected dogs do not always find their way to the statistics.

Misdiagnoses is also a common problem. It is easy to assume 'idiopathic', particularly in breeds known for it. Very often aggression has its roots elsewhere - the most common being in fear and dominance.

There is no treatment barring euthanasia. In rare cases there could be a link to epilepsy therefore the use of anti-convulsant drugs might have some effect. But, if dogs are displaying the behaviour, with no clinical connections, then euthanasia is the only answer.

Competitive Aggression

This occurs when two animals are in such a similar position in the hierarchy that they cannot easily determine which is 'top dog'. They are usually of the same age, sex and size. It is very common among siblings, but equally can occur with others that fit the criteria.

It is more common in breeds that have been bred to work singly, and less common in breeds that are bred to work together such as hounds.

The dog often directs competitive aggression to children as he sees them as rivals, whereas he may well see the adults in the family as higher ranking.

Preventing & Treating Competitive Aggression

It is always difficult to get owners to look at this from the dog's point of view. Most people tend to favour the underling when in fact this will exasperate the situation.

- The dogs should not be treated equally. The owner needs to determine which is the more dominant and favour that one first. Favour comes in the form of feeding, petting and indeed in all situations the more dominant it given priority. This will widen the social gap and leave less necessity for the dogs to compete against each other.
- It should also be noted that position can change as dogs grow older or mature. With the introduction of a new dog into a family, it could be that initially the older dog is dominant, but gradually the younger takes over the 'Alpha' role. Owners must move with this natural change and always favour the current leader.
- The dog needs to know its place in the ranking and children need to be educated in how to take high ranking positions. (*See dominance rules*).

Possessive Aggression

This can be linked with competitive and dominant aggression and if so the rules above apply. It is a general term given when a dog is aggressive over possessions, e.g. beds, toys or bones. Really it is a form of dominance and should be treated as such. Possessive behaviour can also be seen displayed over people.

Some bitches become possessive during pregnancy, and litter rearing, or during a false (pseudo) pregnancy. Again this is linked to dominance and if the bitch truly knew her place in the hierarchy she would not display this behaviour.

Protective Aggression

Protective aggression can be motivated by fear or triggered by dominance. It is inherited, learnt or can be a combination of the two. This is why certain breeds are easier to train for guarding than others. If these breeds are not correctly socialised then they are more likely to protect their territory or possessions in an inappropriate or uncontrolled way.

Some females display protective aggression during litter rearing or in false pregnancy over pseudo puppies, although this is normally termed maternal aggression.

Preventing and Treating Protective Aggression

Avoid confrontations. Withdraw rewards and bring out only for counter conditioning which needs to be applied. Also teach basic control exercises to gain better overall control of the dog.

Maternal Aggression

Displayed by females during pregnancy or pseudo pregnancy, and litter rearing. In fact it is more often the case that the aggression arises when there are no puppies. Production of the female hormone progesterone is responsible for this seemingly irrational behaviour. The bitch becomes possessive over 'surrogate' puppies. This can be a toy, an old rag, a piece of bedding - in fact anything the bitch cares to deem 'her puppy'.

The behaviour will often last the same length as the pregnancy would have. If a litter is produced the behaviour may last a further two months.

Prevention & Treatment of Maternal Aggression

While the behaviour does have its roots in hormones, there is also an element of dominance or fear related reactions involved. Bitches who are well down in the pecking order at home are less likely to exhibit this sort of behaviour as are females who feel confident and not threatened by their owners.

If they do become maternally aggressive, they should be jollied along. Take time to make friends with the bitch before trying to touch the puppy, whether real or imaginary. At first do not pick the pup up straight away, and when you do, stroke it then go back to the bitch using small soothing talk to reassure her.

Territorial Aggression

Territorial aggression is largely an inherited tendency. It happens in both males and females and usually becomes evident at around the time of puberty.

Territory can be defined in a number of ways, it can include the home, gardens, yard, car and indeed any other area the dog deems his territory. Sometimes this extends to public areas where the dog is regularly exercised.

A typical example is when the dog shows aggression to a delivery person such as the postman. The show of aggression works in the dog's mind because the 'intruder' soon retreats. Thus the behaviour is rewarding because it is successful.

Prevention & Treatment of Territorial Aggression

Counter conditioning works the best. The dog needs to learn that all these visitors are friendly and not a threat.

- Withdraw rewards, toys and petting. The owner needs to be a little withdrawn too. Most owners are very doting and the dog tends to get attention whenever it dictates.

- Teach the dog that the owner is in control of treats and all aspects of the dog's daily life.
- Set up situations to counter condition.
- Rewards and petting can be then given in the company of visitors.
- Encourage visitors to reward the dog with treats.
- Avoid confrontations that cannot be controlled until counter conditioning is successful.
- Reward the dog for good behaviour.

Predatory Aggression

Predatory aggression is genetic, all dogs are predators and therefore have the potential to become aggressive in this context, but some have a much stronger prey drive than others. It is usually displayed when chasing an animal of another species; typically rabbits, squirrels, sheep etc., but it can also be used on children.

Some breeds have been developed by man to exhibit this behaviour even more, terriers and greyhounds are prime examples. Ex racing greyhounds pose a particular problem.

Preventing and Treating Predatory Aggression

Predatory is perhaps the most difficult type of aggression to treat because to chase and kill is so natural to the dog. It is the way his ancestors survived, and he still maintains their genes. Counter conditioning can work if the problem is mild or detected early enough. But, once the problem has got a hold it is difficult to find a reward that will motivate the dog sufficiently to leave his prey.

Often the handler's overall control and bond with the dog is not sufficient to maintain the dog's interest and therefore this predatory behaviour is far more desirable to the dog. Once overall control has been achieved, and strong bonding exists between handler and dog, carefully controlled counter-conditioning can work very effectively.

Trainers have been known to use electric shock treatment on these cases, but there are many problems associated with this, (*see equipment*), with the advances in behavioural therapy and the wealth of knowledge and techniques available, it is better and more humane to devise a control system that will prevent and control the behaviour. In the meantime the dog can be exercised away from livestock or on an extending lead.

In the case of dogs who have previously been allowed or worse trained to chase and kill the behaviour, even if counter conditioned, can never be relied up on.

Learned Aggression

This may well be linked to any of the above. The animal learns to be aggressive as a canine solution to a situation that he finds himself in. Initially this aggression may come under any of the above categories, but once the animal is using this strategy it is also becoming a learnt behaviour.

The services use learned aggression in their training, for example the police dog. He is taught to catch a criminal and on the same shift may be required to allow a child to pet him, therefore the criminal attack is usually taught by the retrieve exercise, extending to retrieving a soft sleeve and then onto the sleeve while it is on the trainer's arm. In conjunction with this he is taught to 'leave' and to 'Speak' (bark), the police dog handler can then control the dog using a display of mock learned aggression and the 'Speak' to catch his criminal.

Some dogs are trained to fight (although this is illegal) as in the case of Pitbulls etc., and often pain is used to induce aggression. Also some of this behaviour is passed down via genetics.

Preventing and Treating Learned Aggression

Prevention is always difficult if the owner is not expecting aggression as a result of certain actions. But, avoiding any circumstance that can provoke an aggressive act will avoid the learning taking place and/or put the situation under control until a solution can be sort.

Hurting a dog in an attempt to stop aggression or a fight - in most cases - will make things worse. Shock treatment is a better medium, (e.g. a bucket of water, water power hose, loud noise), but extreme caution must be used, it is so easy for the dog to make the wrong connection.

Learned aggression is better treated in a similar way to other problematic behaviours by controlled counter-conditioning.

Special Needs

Sometimes you will have to deal with specific special needs. Obviously if these involve behavioural problems then the route for treatment is set out in that section, but what of the other problems that affect a surprising number of dogs and their owners?

Special Canine Needs

Deafness

Deafness is alarmingly common in dogs. Quite a high proportion of white dogs are born deaf. It is also a common problem for older dogs, as the body degenerates hearing is often one of the first things to go. In older dogs the loss is usually reasonably gradual and, at the first sign, handlers can start to adjust training and handling to include signals that later the dog will learn to rely on.

Training a deaf dog will require a different approach and yet the rules are still the same. The dog needs to be taught in a way that he can understand. Therefore, the best way is with a variety of signals instead of keywords. A good idea is to teach the dog a signal that means pay attention to me, this signal is followed up with a reward, so that the dog learns that it is fun and rewarding to pay attention. The handler should be encouraged to touch the dog and have certain touch signals that get messages across.

Deaf dogs can be trained quite well to a target stick, this is especially useful when training smaller dogs, as it gives an extension to the handler's arm. Of course the clicker is not much use, but the dog soon learns to touch the target for a reward without the sound of a clicker to help him. (See *Clicker and target training*).

Facial expression, touch and body posture are all the more important in the training of a deaf dog, and handlers must be made aware of how these aspects can be used.

Of course there are safety issues to consider. It must be remembered that, if the deaf dog is not looking in the right direction he will not get the message from the handler, therefore if he is not focused on the handler he must be on lead in a public area or anywhere that he might endanger himself or others.

Perhaps the most important aspect of training a deaf dog is that the owner must have a very good bond with the dog - the dog must **want** to look at his owner.

Blindness

It is less common to be confronted with a young blind dog than a young deaf dog, as blindness is most commonly linked with the onset of age in dogs, any blind puppies are usually euthanased.

Elderly dogs grow accustomed to dealing with the problem, as it gradually comes upon them. It is important to keep life as normal as possible by keeping furniture in the same places, and not leaving things around that the dog can run into. Unlike a blind person, a blind dog may not always be aware of his disability and may try to run around in areas that he feels are safe. So handlers must learn to be the dog's eyes and to make sure the environment is safe for their pet.

Sudden occurrence of blindness, and even partial sight loss due to injury or illness can be more traumatic. It may take a dog quite a while to grow accustomed to his lack of sight. Once again the handler must be the dog's eyes, and also use their voice to guide.

If a dog looses the sight of one eye it is easy for the handler to assume he will adjust, but of course the dog cannot think like we do. He may be taken unawares by things coming from his blind side, this can cause fear, panic and even aggression in a previously sound dog. The handler can help the dog by turning him to face things so that he can see, before he is startled. Also help him to use his hearing more, make sure there are no noisy chains or discs around his neck as these will mask other sounds and will distract him.

The techniques for training the blind dog are just the same as any other dog, he will follow a titbit using his keen sense of smell, or you can use a combination of modelling (placing the dog into positions) and treats to help him to learn. Clicker training can also be beneficial, the sound becomes very reassuring, but of course he needs much more guidance and control than a sighted dog.

Both Deaf and Blind

To have a dog who is both deaf and blind is highly unusual, but it does happen. Use what is left. Sense of smell, guidance with hands and lead. Check the hearing (there may be a tiny bit of hearing), try a whistle with differing pitches etc. Or for sight, try a flashlight to see if there is any reaction, or perhaps different colours.

A combination of modelling and treat luring is the best approach to training, and touch signals will have to be devised. The handler may also master sit, down, stand and heel using a titbit lure because the deaf/blind dog can of course follow scent, he can even learn to recall from the garden to the scent of his favourite treat. Keep it in a sealed container and open it to release the aroma when you want him back.

Deaf/blind dogs often move in a circle, and detect movement or presence of others by air change and scent. Once again the handler must be the dog's eyes and ears, and make sure that their environment is safe. Off lead work, except in a very safe area, is not recommended.

Physical Disabilities

In a dog this usually means the loss of a leg, or the damage, degeneration or deformity of joints, limbs or feet. Obviously some positions may be uncomfortable for the animal, and therefore the dog should be allowed and encouraged to take up those that are more comfortable.

Work with the dog and handler to get the best for them, look for alternatives where appropriate.

Work on the dog's strong points and work out exercises that can strengthen the parts of the body that are effective and may need to take the stress and strain of the disability.

Special Human Needs

Disabilities

Nowadays there are many organisations who are set up to help disabled dog owners, and some will even help the disabled dog owner to teach their own dog to be of great help in the home.

If at all possible it would be best to let the experts deal with these cases, particularly in the cases of severe disabilities, but if it has to be left to you, take time to talk to the owner, assess the dog and to find the best methods of teaching the team. There are always many techniques of teaching a dog, and you should be able to adapt something to suit.

Sometimes handlers are affected by minor difficulties, perhaps the inability to bend, frailty, or other infirmities. Once again each person must be dealt with as an individual. There are many pieces of equipment that may help to give the owner better control, for example head collars, walking harness, extending leads and so on.

The concept of shaping behaviours, clicker and target training will be of great benefit to many, as the dog is required to do more work than the handler, and the patient handler will reap great results from the motivated dog.

Once the owner gains a certain level of control, the dog will start to become their helper instead of hindering. The dog can be trained to pick things up, open and close doors, take things from one person to another, pull out laundry - the possibilities are endless.

Deaf Handlers

Deaf handlers should be treated exactly as everyone else, except you must make sure that you understand the way they 'hear'. They may lip-read, use hearing aids, signing or a combination of these.

In all cases you should make sure that you are always facing them when talking, and make sure that they are looking at you when you are giving instructions. They, just like everyone else, will be distracted by the dog, but unlike others if they are not looking at you they may not be hearing.

Even if using hearing aids, they may have difficulty with the acoustics of the hall, general noise around them or if outside, wind or rain etc. Try to seat them in a quiet area. Hearing aids pick up the nearest sound first and if this is a chatting couple or a noisy dog, they will become frustrated with themselves, the dog and you!

You may find it useful and helpful to devise special signals for the handler when they are taking part in class exercises. Learning a few BSL signs will also go down well - even if it is just a few well chosen signs like 'hello'.

Teaching Children

Children should always be encouraged to take a part in class, and the good instructor will help families to enjoy their pet.

There are lots of ways of improving the dog and child's relationship, as well as increasing the dog's chance of survival, by educating children in the right ways to approach, train and react to dogs. If children know how to react and behave around dogs, it is far more likely that the dog will behave in a suitable manner around children.

As is often said, children can be cruel, and dogs are sometimes the victims of this. However, well educated children will take delight in training the dog instead of making up their own games.

Even a toddler, with the support of an instructor or parent, can control the largest of dogs. Using a titbit the child can lure the dog into sit, down and stand and will be able to get him to follow at heel.

It should not be recommended that a child be left alone with the dog, or encouraged to

Take time to assist children with the training of the dog

185

take a large dog (or any size that they cannot both physically and mentally control), out in a public area, but at the same time controlled sessions will be of great benefit to all.

The child should also be taught how to get the dog to leave and to not jump up. These are important exercises that will give the child control.

Feeding time is a time when many parents keep their children away from the dog, but they should be encouraged to feed and control the dog's food. While it may not be a problem to start with it could soon become one. (*See problem behaviours - dominance*)

Control of toys is often a difficult area, many children are accustomed to having their toys strewn around the house and when a pup comes along, he has a great time. It is a good idea to set some rules. The child has certain areas where the dog is not allowed, and here toys can be on the floor. In other areas toys are not allowed to be left lying around to tempt the dog. The dog learns to leave on command. The dog has toys of his own, but the humans - including the child have control of these.

If a child is chastised, the dog should be put out of the way so that he cannot see this as a chance to work on his position in the hierarchy.

One of the most common problems associated with children (and some adults), is waving their hands around in an attempt to stroke the head of the animal. They should be encouraged to hold out the flat of their hand for the dog to sniff, and then to stroke the chest or to the side of the dog's neck until the dog is confident in the child.

Shrill voices tend to excite dogs. Children should be taught to use quiet voices around dogs, and in fact all animals. It is good training for children to learn to adjust their manner for the benefit of another, even if it is just a dog. In turn the dog will reward the child with love and affection that is second to none.

If a child is frightened of dogs it is a good idea to take him to areas where other children will pet a calm, well controlled dog. Often they can be encouraged to touch the back of the dog - this is easier than facing the front end with all of those teeth! Once they see others communicating well, they may start to overcome their fear. Of course if the fear is as a result of being bitten, getting over this will take sometime and patience from all concerned. The child has to want to overcome the fear and should not be pushed, just set a good example and allow the child to go at their own speed.

Natural Therapies

Sometimes, training and behaviour problems can be given a helping hand with some natural therapy. You don't have to be an expert to use and see the beneficial effects that can be reaped from the correct choice and use of natural products and procedures.

Touch Therapy

Pioneered by Linda Tellington Jones from the USA, 'Touch Therapy' can be used to calm, refresh and even enhance the dog's capacity to learn. It promotes good natural posture, it is non-confrontational and encourages the dog and also the handler to relax and learn without stress. It comprises of gentle massage and posture control as well as a range of training techniques that can help all dogs including those who are difficult.

In order to carry out the therapies, the handler must have physical contact with the dog. This in itself is a great boost to the relationship between dog and handler and therefore promotes success.

Linda has written a great book, (*see reading list*), that is a must for all dog training instructors.

Bach Remedies

The Bach remedies were developed by Dr Edward Bach (pronounced Batch). These remedies are made from the flowers of wild plants, trees and bushes. Dr Bach died in 1936, he was a physician and a homeopath, he spent his life searching for the purest methods of healing and the 'medicines' that he developed are still in use today.

The remedies consist of 38 different types, each one for a specific situation. Also there is one, 'Rescue Remedy', that is made up of five different medicines and is designed to help us cope with particularly difficult or demanding situations.

The medicines can be used for depression, anxiety and other emotional factors and can have beneficial effects for both humans and animals. Many dog trainers have reported beneficial results following the use of these remedies in conjunction with training programmes.

The book, 'The Work of Dr Edward Bach', explains the remedies and how to use them, (*see reading list*).

Homeopathy

Homeopathic medicine is based on the philosophy that any substance which can cause symptoms of an illness can also be used in the treatment. Therefore homeopathy experts match the two to achieve their results. The medicines all come from natural sources

There are many helpful books on homeopathy, as well as a number of people who specialise in treating animals for a variety of complaints and disorders (both physical and mental).

Herbal Medicine

As the name suggests, herbal medicine uses the merits of plants, and only plants, to treat its patients. It is often confused with homeopathy but the difference is that homeopathy uses plant, animal and mineral to gain its affect.

Other Therapies

There are a number of other therapies including acupuncture, physiotherapy etc., but these really do require expert practitioners. Forward thinking vets can give you contacts in your area or you may find recommendation by word of mouth.

Definition of Terms

When embarking in the field of behaviour and training of dogs many terms are used. This section gives brief definitions of most of the commonly and some of the less commonly used terms. If the term you require is not here it may be covered in its own section for example a list of different types of aggression are covered in the chapter on behavioural problems.

Adaptation - The animal adjusts to an environment, so he may survive or benefit.

Alarm Reaction - Prepares the animal for fight or flight by increased blood pressure, heart rate and absorption and conversion of sugars etc.

Anthropomorphic - Giving human characteristics to animals and other non human entities.

Anticipation - A state of readiness for a specific event or exercise.

The term is also used to refer to unwanted anticipation, i.e. the animal goes into the pattern of behaviour that it has learnt before the signal is given, sometimes in an inappropriate way.

Anxiety - A stressful, emotional or affective state resulting from the anticipation of danger, punishment or unpleasant (perceived or real) occurrences. High levels of anxiety interferes with all aspects of learning.

Appeasement Gestures - These are signals or behaviours that the dog offers to people or other animals that he sees as higher in the pecking order than himself. They are given to signal that the dog is not to be taken as a threat. These gestures included: paw lifting, lip licking, rolling over, head turning and other submissive or calming behaviours.

Associated Learning - Learning which has resulted from the direct linking of a stimulus with a response. Pavlovian (Classical) and Operant conditioning are examples of associative learning procedures.

Attachment - The secure relationship (tie or bond) which develops between mother and offspring, puppy and breeder, dog and trainer/owner etc. The attachment figure is seen as a protector against environmental stress and in turn the dog attempts to keep the attachment figure close.

Automatic Behaviour - Well practised responses which have been pushed from the forefront of consciousness. This then allows the animal higher levels of decision making and problem solving as he does not need to think about the response that has become automatic.

Avoidance Learning - Operant procedure where an unpleasant or punishing event is avoided by the animal behaving in a specific way.

Behaviour Chain - A series of behaviours where each one is rewarded by the opportunity to do the next. Normally trained backwards so that the animal can always see reward following a behaviour. Requires good timing, careful handling and should be set up to ensure animal is rewarded at the right time.

Bite Inhibition - The dog learns to inhibit the intensity of his bite, usually in early puppy hood, when he plays with his siblings and at a stage when his jaws cannot do too much damage. If he bites too hard then the other pups will withdraw and not want to play, therefore he learns quickly to inhibit his bite. Should be continued when the pup goes into his human home. Humans should take the place of the litter mates, withdrawing play when the pup bites too hard. Teaching the pup that human flesh is not to be bitten.

Calming Signals - Signals given by the dog that are intended to calm others and 'switch off' anger or pressure. Signals include submissive behaviours, head turning, circling, displacement behaviours. Also physically going between animals in conflict

Classical Conditioning - The theory generally connected with the work of the Russian scientist Ivan Pavlov. An involuntary response to a stimulus that the animal has learnt the concept of. It is termed a 'visceral' reaction. Pavlov classically conditioned his dogs to salivate at the sound of a bell which he had followed up with the feeding of meat powder.

Competency Motivation - Animals can become motivated by tasks or exercises that they have learnt, show a general interest and be motivated by them. (Training becomes self motivating)

Conditioning - The process of learning the relationship between stimuli and response.

Conditioned Reflex - The response acquired and given automatically to a stimulus. For example Pavlov's famous dogs. The bell became a conditioned stimulus to which the dogs salivated. The salivation is the conditioned reflex.

Conditioned Reinforcer - Something that becomes the signal to the animal that a reward is coming i.e. "the behaviour you are doing when you hear, feel, smell or see your conditioned reinforcer, is the correct one". A good example of a conditioned reinforcer is the 'Clicker'.

Conditioned Response - An action taught, inadvertently taught, or otherwise learnt by the animal as a response to a given signal, word or set of circumstances.

Conditioned Stimulus - A word, sound or signal that the animal has been conditioned to and comes to understand as a given meaning. After training has successfully taken place, the keyword 'Sit' is the conditioned stimulus that make the dog understand that he should sit when he hears it.

Counter Conditioning - A method of retraining. Teaching the animal an alternative behaviour to the one that he is presenting by putting the new behaviour under command and reinforcing with a powerful incentive such as an exciting toy or cooked liver. Then the stimulus that caused the previous behaviour is introduced in a mild fashion but, before the dog has chance to react, the new preferred behaviour is encouraged and rewarded.

Cue - Signal, sound or circumstances that the animal has come to associate with a given behaviour or series of behaviours.

Desensitisation - A method of retraining to make the dog less sensitive to an object, procedure or situation etc. For example, the animal is taught to calmly accept a stimulus that previously frightened him. The object of the animal's fear can be presented in a less fearful way while the dog is kept under control. The intensity is raised as the animal becomes desensitised. Animals can be inadvertently desensitised to stimulus that is desirable, e.g. many handlers repeat commands and accept the animals unresponsive attitude to the command - thus desensitising the dog to that command.

Drives - This refers to behavioural tendencies that the dog has inherited from his ancestors. They split into three areas; pack drive, prey drive and defence drive.

Dogs can be assessed by means of their most commonly high rating drives and trained with this in mind. The depth of drive will affect their personality:

Pack drive - dogs high in behaviours that involve contact with others, likes to be at home is unlikely to wander except to reproduce. It is the sort of dog that follows you around in the home, enjoys being petted and groomed. Pack life is important to these dogs, they may well be unhappy when left alone. They are very sensitive to body language. Also dogs high in pack drive are likely to have strong reproductive behaviours.

Prey drive - Dogs high in prey drive activities like to chase, shake and play tug games. They enjoy tearing and ripping apart a variety of items. Digging and burying is great fun. They are likely to jump up a lot, bark (often high pitched and excitable). They keenly use their senses of hearing, sight and scent

Defence Drive - This can be broken down into two sections - 'defence fight' and 'defence flight'. Fight signs can be seen in dogs that stand tall and stand their ground. They may also display dominant type behaviours like food, territory and toy guarding. He may dislike being petted and refuse to be moved. Flight dogs are unsure of themselves and easily run and hide from a variety of situations. Flight dogs may also use the 'freeze' technique, i.e. they will keep still not going forward of backwards, this is a defence against perceived possible predators.

Displacement Behaviour - These are behaviours that are carried out when the dog is feeling under pressure or is unsure of what to do next. The behaviour gives the dog temporary relief and some thinking time to assess the situation. The behaviour is usually unrelated to the situation. Displacement behaviours could be any behaviour the dog sees as a diversion, but most displacements include behaviours such as yawning, scratching, stretching and sniffing.

Extinction - The reduction of a learned response that occurs when the stimulus controlling it is repeatedly presented without reinforcement being given. For example ignoring, failing to reward, preventing, manipulating circumstances to eliminate or issuing 'time out' will make a behaviour less desirable to perform and so will lead to extinction. Frequency of the behaviour will drop to its naturally occurring level.

Flooding - The animal's mind is flooded with something until he learns to ignore or disregard it.

Force Methods - Linked to negative reinforcement, the dog is forced by means of punishment being given when he does not conform to the trainer's ideal. The dog learns to avoid punishment by performing the desired response. Punishment can vary from mild reprimand to severe abuse. However planned, this style of teaching puts pressure on the recipient which slows down the overall learning process, even though it may seem to speed up the initial response. Also it is easy for the trainer to loose their temper because they are already in a negative frame of mind.

Generalisation - Many animals will learn to generalise, i.e. 'cue' means do something - 'no cue' means do nothing. Different cues mean do different things. 'Hold', initially means the first item trained but eventually means 'Hold' any item offered in the same way.

Habit - A learned sequence of behaviours stimulated by a variety of messages.

Habituation - Learning to ignore stimuli that are without significance. Prolonged exposure or gradual introduction to something, making it a normal or acceptable thing for the animal. Using this methods requires gentle or remote introductions to start with and then gaining intensity to the desired end. Usually used in conjunction with reward or other common bond. i.e. something the animal associates as good or desired for best results.

Inherit - Characteristics gained through genetics.

Innate - Present at birth - not learned.

Instant Reaction - Animal reacts instantly to a learned stimuli.

Instinct - A pattern of behaviour which is common to all members of a species and has not been learnt.

Intelligence - Very difficult to define and really should be used in relative terms, e.g. relative to breed, age, circumstances and past experience etc. It is also relative to species and motivation. Intelligence reflects the ability to learn, think and understand, relating to the quality and complexity of tasks etc.

Mental Sensitivity - Linked to the animal's ability to handle stress. A mentally sensitive animal is more likely to suffer anxiety related problems.

Modelling - Techniques used in training which involve physically manipulating the animal into position, for example using hands and lead to get the dog into a sit position.

Motivation - The energy behind behaviour. Usually measured by the dog's willingness to work and learn.

Natural Methods - Linked to positive reinforcement, the dog is not forced into required behaviour, moreover he is guided and rewarded to make him want to display the behaviour that will illicit a reward. Also use of drives, body language and therapeutic techniques to achieve aims.

Negative Reinforcement - To make it unpleasant for an animal to carry out (or not too carry out) a certain behaviour. Inflicting pain on an animal must highlight the welfare issue and therefore this technique is generally unacceptable and counter productive. However, negative reinforcement can be used effectively by withdrawing the training session when applying the Skinnerian theory (*See Shaping*).

Neotenize - To retain youthful and playful behaviour. We have selectively bred to retain playfulness in our dogs, we can capitalise on the dog's ability to learn through play.

Observational learning - Behaviours learnt by observing the behaviour of others. The earliest and commonest way of learning.

Operant Conditioning/Learning - A type of conditioning of the animal's mind based on work carried out by B. F. Skinner. Skinner worked on rats which he kept in boxes. They were trained to do things for reward. A certain action is carried out by the animal and is strengthened (or weakened) as a result of the events that follow that response. Used in training the required response is followed up by reward. Ideal training method for behaviours that occur naturally or can be set up. The trainer controls the stimuli, rewards and therefore the responses.

Pheromone - A sort of social signal given off as a scent, e.g. the scent given off by a female on heat.

Positive Reinforcement - The strength and frequency of a behavioural response is increased because the dog is rewarded for a correct response - all other responses are ignored, blocked or guided against.

Primary Reinforcer - The incentive that the animal is primarily working for - often food or play. However a secondary reinforcer, such as a signal to say that the food is coming, can become just as important to the animal.

Punishment - Can be anything that the dog attempts to escape or avoid. Can be physical pain, intimidation, fear, lack of contact. The best form of punishment to compliment modern methods of training is ostracism, rewards are withheld, the dog is instantly ignored or withdrawn from when he misbehaves.

Random Reward - Animals are given rewards intermittently with no set pattern. They consequently learn that a reward will come but they are not sure when. This strengthens a behaviour as the animal will try harder to instigate the reward.

Reflex - An involuntary, automatic and mechanical response to a stimulus without the involvement of higher cerebral processes. A behaviour that the animal does not think about.

Reinforcer - A means of encouraging (or discouraging) a behaviour.

Reward - Something the animal works towards receiving. Can be food, touch, play, attention, sound, freedom, sex or in fact anything the animal desires.

Secondary Reinforcer - A signal to say that the primary reinforcer is coming. A clicker is a secondary reinforcer, food usually being the primary reinforcer.

Self Motivating - (See competency motivation)

Selective Attention - Concentration on a stimulus or event to the exclusion of others.

Shaping - New behaviours are put under trainer control through the rewarding of those behaviours when they occur, or when they are induced. Once the responses are established, only those behaviours which approximate more closely to the final goal are reinforced, i.e. the behaviour is 'shaped' nearer and nearer to the final goal by rewarding behaviours. Then, as the animal progresses, the trainer ceases to reward lesser behaviours and rewards only those that are nearer the desired target. Once an improvement is made, only this is rewarded and the previously mediocre attempts are ignored. (*See chapter on clicker training*).

Sight Sensitivity - The animal's reaction level to objects or animals seen. Sight sensitive dogs very soon pick up the slightest movement.

Sound Sensitivity - An animals degree of response to sound.

Stimulus - Something that acts as an incentive or trigger. A keyword can be a stimulus and so is food.

Stimulus Control - A behaviour can be said to be under stimulus control when it occurs only on the introduction of the stimulus.

Stress - The effect of being subjected to an unpleasant or undesirable event or situation (perceived or real).

Superstitious Behaviour (Passive training) - When an animal is picking up a cue or reinforcement from the environment that is nothing to do with the training - but is a constant feature or an accidental occurrence. For instance, in training the handler may be following a set pattern, the dog picks up on the pattern, thus being unable to understand how to perform unless the handler follows the same pattern.

Submission - (Active) An animal submits to another animal or person's wishes but, his body language does not show classic signs of submission, i.e. the body remains in a normal stature, and the animal may indeed be vocal. For example, when a dog is told by his owner to get off a piece of furniture, he does so but remains actively alert with upright body stance and with no visible signs of submission. A very active submission may include lively vocalisations.

Active submission would also be the case if he stood his ground in an excited way neither submitting or challenging. However, it should be remembered that the reason for apparent disobedience is often lack of understanding.

Submission - (Passive) An animal submits to another and shows the signs of submission in its body posture. For example, a dog is told by its owner to get off a piece of furniture, it does so and shows other signs of submission i.e. low body posture, head turning and perhaps submissive urination. Some passive submitters will be so submissive that they are unable to move from the spot, lying on their backs, exposing underside, lifting legs etc. Therefore this could, (but should not) be construed as disobedience, the dog is merely attempting to turn off the pressure from the owner.

Successive Approximation - The art/science of shaping a behaviour. Gradually raising the criteria, rewarding only those behaviours that 'successively approximate' (get nearer to) the target behaviour, ceasing to reward lesser behaviours, so extinguishing them. (*See Shaping*).

Superstitious Behaviour - Animals pick up signals that are not really relevant to the task but, have been present during training, and therefore deemed to be part of the task. For example a dog trained to sit in close proximity to a red bucket may think that the action is required only when the red bucket is there.

Systematic Desensitisation - The animal is gradually and systematically exposed to something so that he becomes blasé to it.

Touch Sensitivity - How sensitive an animal is to touch or pain. Often tested by squeezing the skin between the animal's toes with increasing pressure to a count of 10, this test is used in puppy assessment testing at around 6 -7 weeks of age.

Traditional Methods - Usually refers to methods using compulsion, negative reinforcement and restraint rather than the sole use of positive reinforcement, guidance and motivation.

Trial and Error Learning - A type of learning in which the animal tries out a number of responses to a given stimulus until it hits upon one which produces the desired effect.

Triggers - Stimuli that set off or provoke a behaviour. Triggers can be the sight, sound, smell or touch of an object, animal or environment etc. Triggers can be taught or otherwise learnt.

Voluntary Behaviour - A behaviour which is intended by the animal.

Appendix 1

Most Important Aspects of Being a Good Dog Owner Handler

Attributes of the hander -
Patience. Pleasant calm attitude. Understanding. Compassion.
Controlled You must have complete control
            The dog must know you are in control

How is this Achieved?
        Look at things from the dog's point of view
        Concentrate on the dog
        Read the dog's body language and signals
        Apply suitable techniques and equipment
        Use equipment correctly and humanly
        Motivate and reward correct behaviours
        Guide away from or block problem behaviours
        Don't allow problem behaviours to reoccur
        Don't blame the dog for errors
        Train step by step
        Train in many differing environments
        Anticipate the dog's reactions
        Anticipate distractions
        Be adaptable ready to change when necessary
        Be aware of your dog's response and its meaning
        Communicate with the animal
        Be fair

Reproduced with permission of © IABTC Angela White 1999

General Do's and Don'ts

Don't worry if your dog does not get the idea of what you want straight away but, if he seems very confused, look to your teaching and timing rather than blaming the dog. It may be something as simple as your hand position that confuses him. If your training is sound, you should see some improvement quite quickly.

Do train in differing environments. The dog will not necessarily know that you mean the same thing in different surroundings unless you teach him this in a pleasant, positive manner.

Don't introduce a word for an action until you have perfected the training technique and can successfully get the dog into the required position, otherwise he will be learning to ignore the word rather than obey it!

Do have an open mind and learn as much as you can about your dog, this will help you and your dog to enjoy life together to the full.

Don't assume that once you have trained a few exercises, the training is done. To keep good control you should train on a regular basis, and apply at least some of your techniques as part of a daily routine. Little and often is the best way to learn.

Do groom your dog at least twice a week, (more if his coat needs it), even if he is a smooth coated dog. Grooming is an important social exercise and will help you to control your dog's behaviour as well as allow you to detect any problems that might need professional treatment.

Don't allow your dog to dictate what happens in your day-to-day life, or in your training. Remember who is controlling who!

Do use reward based training methods and reward while the dog is performing the task.

Don't reward or reprimand after the dog has performed, he will not connect your attention to the correct item of behaviour if you do.

Do enjoy your training, the task should be fun for you, your family, and the dog.

Don't loose your temper, anger shows lack of control. The dog, like a child will not learn readily or perform accurately under pressure.

Do keep calm and handle your animal with compassion. He has few free choices in his life of domesticity - you have many!

Reproduced with permission of © IABTC Angela White 1999

198

Dog School Homework

Week One

Background Information

One of the most important things about bringing up your dog correctly is taking care of his training. A trained dog is a pleasure to own. He will have a more enjoyable lifestyle because he will know his place, and of course can be allowed much more freedom than that of an untrained dog.

In order to get the best results it is important to make sure that your pet is fit and healthy. He should enjoy a good quality suitable diet. He should be given exercise appropriate for his age and size. You cannot expect your dog to perform well unless he feels well.

It is also important that your training is put over to the dog in a way that he can understand. To be affective at this, every dog owner should understand just a little about how the dog's mind works.

The dog's memory works in a different way to ours, in that he reacts to situations as they happen. His reactions are governed by his previous experiences, his instincts, his hormones and other bodily functions. All animals, and dogs are not any different, are driven by two main motivators, these are food and sex! It makes sense, therefore, to use one of these motivators to our advantage in the training of our faithful friend. Of course it is not easy to use sex, though we should be well aware of its power, therefore we look to food as the best tool.

Dogs are predatory animals, and in their development, play behaviours have a dominant role in the learning process. Therefore, it follows that play can be just as good a motivator as food, if used in the correct way.

Like humans, if a dog gets too much of a good thing, all but the most obsessive types will get bored or sickened. Giving controlled amounts, at just the right time, will get the best results. For example, the dog is told to sit, he does so, and then he is allowed to move, if the reward comes after he has moved, even seconds after, then the dog will associate the reward for the movement and not for the sit. This concept applies to all training, and also needs to be applied when things go wrong.

If the dog is carrying out a behaviour that you do **not** want, it is no use chastising him **after** the event. Even moments after he will no longer connect your reprimand to the incorrect behaviour. You may feel that he does understand, because he will be subdued, but in fact he will be reacting only to your attitude. Therefore, if your dog is doing something wrong, you should either catch him in the act, and correct him by creating either a physical barrier or using a verbal command of 'No' or 'Leave', (if you have developed your training effectively). Better still, set up training situations and teach him the correct reactions in a positive way.

Having a kind and positive attitude to your training will show the dog that you are in control, and he will respect you far more than he would if your were aggressive, or lost your temper with him. Correcting behaviour is no where near as effective as teaching the correct behaviour in the first place - prevention is better than cure.

Sit - Start your training by teaching the sit - raise the titbit above your dog's head until he tips back into the sit position. As he does so, say 'sit', in a pleasant, clear tone of voice. Reward the dog while he is in position by giving the titbit, and have another ready to help keep him in position. He may chew at your fingers for the second reward, don't worry, once he has got the idea we will introduce the *'Leave'* exercise to stop this. Just keep him in position for a few seconds, and then break the exercise by giving another keyword *'That'll Do'*. As you say this encourage the dog to move, but do not continue to reward. Use this new skill at various times during the day to gain control of your dog. Many short sessions are better than one long one. A good time to do this is at feed time, or before allowing the dog out of the door, in fact any time that you feel like 'having a go'.

Down - The next exercise to teach is the down. This is a very important exercise as it is also a submissive position, and helps in the control of dominance. Use your titbit again, but this time lower the titbit between the dog's two front paws. You may find it easier to start with him in the sit position, (*as above*), but eventually you will be able to do this from the sit or the stand. Adjust your hand position slowly until you find the correct position to entice the dog into the down position. If you have your hand too far forward he will walk forward toward your hand. It takes practice - don't be afraid to experiment. Once the dog is in the down position, say the new keyword '*Down*', and reward with your titbit, as you did in the sit. Make sure you have another titbit ready to hold his interest and keep him in position, hold him there for a few seconds. Then release as in the sit with your release word, '*That'll Do*', and cease the reward.

Stand - Now you can teach the stand using the same procedure as above, but this time the titbit needs to be in front of the dog at standing nose level. If he is sitting draw him forward into the stand by moving your titbit hand forward in line with the position that his nose will be when he is in the stand, stop moving when he is standing. Introduce your new keyword '*Stand*' as the dog comes into position. Reward and release as above.

Putting it together - Now you can do all three positions, try linking them together. Build up the time in which you keep the dog in each position, but do not become predictable. If the dog starts to know exactly what is coming next he will start to anticipate this, and you will loose the control. Vary the timing of the rewards i.e. do not give a reward every time and avoid creating a pattern that the dog can follow. Repeat this or any separate part of the exercise whenever you have a minute.

Week Two

It is important to carry on training with your dog all the exercises that you learnt last week. You should be able to make progress now. Your dog will stay in each position longer, and will take up the positions much quicker as you get better at the timing and positioning of your rewards as well as the control of your lead. As the dog learns to learn you will find it easier to teach him. If you are still struggling with any of this please ask your instructor for more help.

Leave - This is a very useful thing to teach as it has all sorts of possibilities. If the dog knows the meaning you can tell him to leave all manner of household things, as well as your Sunday roast!

Once again start this training with the dog on his lead. Put the dog in the sit position using your titbit technique. Give him the first titbit and bring the second between your finger and thumb. Tell him '*Leave*'. Once again your tone should be calm and controlled. If he goes forward to try to take the titbit, pull backwards and then release the pressure with a small, gentle tug on your lead, repeat the word '*Leave*'. You may need to repeat this action a few times before he gets the message, especially if you have already done a lot of training with the titbits. As soon as you see an element of success in that he stops straining at the lead, or better still he actively withdraws, reward him with the titbit. Repeat this exercise, building up in small steps and varying the time that he is required to leave, and the distance of the titbit.

Now try placing the titbit on the floor, and with each success bring the next titbit a little closer to the dog. Eventually the dog will leave the titbit, even if it is placed on his own paw! Once you have success, you can then use other things that the dog likes, but is **not** allowed. Put the item in front of him, don't let him touch, (of course keep him on lead so you have good control), and tell him 'Leave'. As soon as he responds correctly reward him with a titbit. Always tell your dog to leave before he has chance to touch things that you treasure. He can't be expected to know unless you tell him!

Week Three

Don't forget - carry on training with your dog all the exercises that you have learnt so far. If you are still struggling with any part of what we have covered so far, please ask your instructor for more help.

Walking by your side - If you are starting out with a young pup, you should never have any problems if you follow this advice. If you have an older dog who has learned to pull, then you will have to be very vigilant. It is a bit like sticking to a healthy diet, you must have the will power to follow it through and stick to the rules for the best results.

To start with choose an area where there are not too many distractions for you and the dog. Put your dog on lead, and stand with him by your side in what would be a comfortable position for you if you were walking with him. Look down at his head position and note where it is. Imagine just in front of him is a brick wall. If he pulls forward at all he will damage his head! Take a step forward, concentrate on the dog, if he goes forward and does not stop in time to save his head from your brick wall, react quickly to save him! Start walking backwards, and guide him back towards you with his lead, keeping him on the same side that he started. Keep guiding him until he goes behind you, and then start to walk forwards again and encourage him to turn, follow you, and come back to your side. When he is back at your side continue forward. Once again if he goes forward from the desired position, repeat the procedure.

Don't introduce any verbal commands, until the dog is getting the idea, just a few murmurs of encouragement as he comes towards you, and again when he comes into position, but nothing when he is incorrect.

Be very careful about your voice control, if you give verbal reward as he comes into position, it is very easy to be still praising as he walks past and goes forward into the wrong position again. It is better to remain silent until he is looking up for your approval in the right place. If your dog is head strong, or is accustomed to pulling, you will have to be extra determined at this stage, but of course you must maintain your pleasant, controlled manner. Soon he will get the message and will be walking happily by your side. An added aid will be to have a titbit in your hand, on the side that the dog is walking so that, as the dog comes into the correct position, he is greeted with an immediate reward.

There will be times, even after the dog has learned what you want, that he will start to pull forward again. For instance, when the dog is excited, or you are in a new environment. Learn to identify these times, and be prepared to work on your control before he gets out of hand.

If you don't want your dog to pull, you will have to decide to prevent it all the time, not just some of the time.

Week Four

Keep practising the Sit, Down, Stand, Leave and Walking to heel on a loose lead. You should be starting to get good results most of the time. Don't go out for a walk and allow your dog to pull at any time, train him like we did in class. If you are struggling with any of this, please ask for help.

Coming Back - Dogs that won't come back can be a danger to others and certainly a great cause of frustration to their owners. If the dog enjoys your company, then coming back will not be a chore. But, if he has learned that it is more fun to sniff trees, hunt out bitches, or pester other people, then he must be taught that the *'new you'* can really be good fun.

If your dog likes playing with toys or enjoys his food, you can use this to your advantage. You should make sure that they are not always available for him, put them all away in a drawer or cupboard, and get them out only when **you** want to play with the dog. This will have the added benefit of helping to keep dominance under control

Decide which toy your dog likes best, and keep this as your special toy. Take him to a quiet place and play with your dog and the toy. Keep him on lead so that you can make sure he comes to you when you call. Throw the toy a few feet, and encourage him to get it, reel him in repeating his name and the word *'come'*, give tiny jerks on the lead, and have an enthusiastic attitude. Repeat this often. You can also use feeding time to encourage the dog to understand the word *'come'*.

Let him go to sniff or be distracted by something, then use his name and your keyword *'come'* and reel him in.

When you have your dog enthusiastically coming to you, introduce your sit command (*see week one*), but this time, touch his collar before you give him his reward. Then allow him to go free again. Now each time he comes and sits, touch his collar and then reward. He will soon learn that this action results in reward and not the end of his fun. Previously he will have come to understand that each time you went to touch his collar it would be the end of the fun i.e. the lead would go on.

Once he is enthusiastically coming, train in a different place so that he gets the idea that you mean the same in varying environments. When you go out, train where there are not too many distractions. Keep calling him back and playing. Bring out the occasional delicious titbit to heighten the enthusiasm.

If you have had problems in the past, your dog will be in the habit of not coming back on command. Use a line, twenty to thirty feet long, attached to his collar. Now you have complete control and you can call him and reel the lead in as above. As the dog's behaviour gets better you can gradually cut off sections, making the line shorter a bit at a time. The dog will associate his new, good behaviour with the line. The last few feet of line should remain attached to the dog for quite some time.

Never chastise your dog for not coming back because **any time** he comes back he is **good**, even if it is after you have been calling for a long time. However, give big rewards for excellent recalls and lesser rewards - say just a stroke of the head if he did not respond straight away.

Week Five

Don't Jump up - This an extremely important exercise for any dog, but even more so with a large dog. If your dog jumps up it could easily knock someone over, probably you but worse, someone who is not accustomed to dogs. To give you control you can incorporate some of the words taught in class, for instance '*sit*'.

If your are teaching a puppy, always go down to the dog to give praise and cuddles - never let the dog jump up to be stroked. If the pup does jump up, gently push him away, stand up straight, turn your back, withdrawing all contact. Then turn back and tell him '*Sit*', use a titbit, or if the pup is starting to understand, a hand signal to help him into position. Reward with praise, strokes and cuddles, only when he has all four feet on the ground. If he tries to raise up again - withdraw or repeat your sit command and signal.

Similar techniques can be used with an adult dog. Turn away if he attempts to jump up. Alternatively you can set up the situation. Put him on lead, allow the dog into the situation where he is likely to jump up, then use your lead to control the dog. Pull firmly downwards and away from your body.

This technique should also be used to stop your dog jumping up at visitors and others. If your dog jumps up when you come in after a time away from him, stand up straight and ignore the dog, have a titbit ready to insist on a sit before you give any attention. Ask visitors to do the same, or control your dog on lead when they come. Make him sit before he is allowed to say "Hello".

A good way of teaching the dog not to jump up is to use the barrier of a gate. Stand the other side of the gate and give him a keyword 'Off'. When he backs off give him a treat as reward. Repeat the process often and try to set up other similar situations to train him. Only reward when he is 'Off'.

Once the dog has jumped up whatever you do afterwards is too late. Always try your best to find ways of preventing the behaviour and this will speed up the learning process.

Week Six

It is very important to keep on training the various exercises that we have covered so far. Therefore start from the beginning and retrain all of the exercises to make sure the dog and you really do have the right idea.

Make sure you train in a variety of situations. Make a point of taking your dog somewhere new this week.

Use what you and your dog have learnt in as many situations as possible. For example, get your dog to 'Sit' before going through the door, having his lead on etc. Use 'Leave' before he eats his dinner, takes a biscuit or picks up something he shouldn't. Use 'Down' when you are grooming, when you want to watch TV, or at bedtime. Use stand to inspect his body, while grooming or when waiting to do something else. The possibilities are endless, just remember all of these exercises have been taught for you to use in your daily life, not just in class or as a training exercise.

Look at your daily routine and right down any problems to report back to class next week.

Use the exercises that you have learned and see if you can teach your dog to do something different to show us next week. It doesn't matter what it is - a trick, a useful exercise or a game.

Appendix 2
Sample Enquiry Letter & Form

Centre for Dog Training

Specialists In Training For Pet, Competition And Problem Dogs
Qualified Instructors With IABTC
Contact:
Address:
Phone:

Thank you for your enquiry about Dog Training. Please find attached a booking form for you to fill in and return as soon as possible to secure your place on the course. Following are some answers to things you may be wondering about, but if there is anything else you would like to know please do not hesitate to contact me. I look forward to meeting you at class.

The Centre's Aim

To promote responsible dog ownership. To help you to train your dog to be a well behaved member of the community, to be an enjoyable family pet, and to help you to achieve your aims and ambitions with training techniques that are kind and enjoyable for both hander and dog.

What Breeds?

All breeds are welcome including crossbreeds.

How Long will it take?

Training is an ongoing process which you will enjoy throughout the dog's life. All dogs, and humans for that matter, learn at differing speeds and start with differing experiences, therefore there is no set time limit. However, everyone who attends regularly and practices at home will see a marked improvement in their dog, and will have a much better understanding of how to achieve their aims and make progress.

Do I Need Special Equipment?

No. Please do not go out a buy a new lead and collar to come training. You will be advised on your first night on the best equipment for you and your dog. The correct training equipment will be on sale at the class, at very competitive prices, or you are free to purchase elsewhere once we have been able to advise you.

Is My Dog Too Young or Old?

Dogs are admitted for training in the puppy class as soon as they are through their inoculations, please do not wait because the earlier you come, the easier it is for us to help you to avoid problems. However, if your dog is older don't worry - it is never too late to start.

What If My Dog Has A Particular Problem?

If you are worried about any aspect of your dog's behaviour in particular please feel free to ring me for a chat before the course starts. Often something that is a problem to you will be normal to deal with for us.

What Shall I Wear?

You will find it more comfortable and safe to wear soft soled, flat shoes or training shoes, and ladies you will find it easier to wear a pair of trousers rather than a skirt.

What Will We Learn?

Our classes are designed to give an insight into dog behaviour and training, and will teach you how to control your dog. This includes; sit, down, stand, leave, walk on a loose lead, come back when called, don't jump up and other social activities. There will be the opportunity to progress further should you wish to, either for competition or just for fun. Individual help will be given on any problems which are specific to you, your family circumstances and your dog, and there will be time allocated for questions and answers.

© AKWhite

Dog Training Class Booking form

Course to be Held at ....
(map enclosed for directions)
Course Title:

Starting on ....for ....weeks

Course fee: £............... per dog for the full ....weeks
    It would be helpful, where possible, if you could turn up a few minutes early to help your dog settle in and take care of any paperwork. Please fill in the attached form and return together with the fee to the address overleaf. Your early response is advisable so that we can reserve a place for you and your dog on the course, places are limited to assure you of our best attention.

Detach Here---

I wish to attend the dog /puppy training course starting on, and enclose the fee.
    I confirm that my dog is fully inoculated, regularly wormed and in good health. I understand that should my dog be in contact with any infectious disease, I will not attend until given the all clear by a vet.

Name...

Address ....

....

Phone (daytime) ....(evening)....................................

Dog's Name..Type of Dog.................................

Sex of Dog......................Is your dog Neutered? Y / N (if so) When...........

Has your dog been ill recently? (give brief details) ....

....

Any Behaviour Problems? Give brief details..

....

Age of Dog............How would you describe its fitness? ....

Are your the first owner?...

Age dog was acquired ....

Where did you get the dog from?...

What do you expect to gain from the course?...

....

Your Dog's Veterinary Surgeon ....

Date................................ Your Signature ....

Method of Payment: Cash/Cheque/Credit Card/PO

(Cheques made payable to: please)

©AKWhite

Appendix 3
Sample Lesson Plan

Date 1st October *Time* 7.00-8.00 *Venue* Dog School
Week No 1 *Group* Beginners *Number Booked* 10

Aim of Lesson - To make clients feel welcome, to assess dogs for potential problems, to check and advise on equipment. To give class basic skills and understanding to get started on control.

Time	Topics	Instructor Activity	Client Activity	Resources Needed	Assessment
7.00	Register Welcome	Seat everyone make checks.	Take time to settle in, meet instructors	Seating clean hall. Titbits, toys spare leads & collars	
7.10	Intro	Explain the course aims - ask for client hopes	Listen, soothe dogs. State hopes for course	Flip chart or large paper and pen to illustrate aims	
7.15	Basics of dog's mind	Explain	Listen		
7.25	Sit, down, stand	Demo	Watch and listen	Demo dog on lead, titbits	
7.30	ditto	Instruct	Have a go		

211

7.40		Explain how to follow up at home	Listen
7.50	Q&A	Lead session with example of common problem	Ask questions re problems at home
7.58	Conclude	Recap on	Listen

Appendix 4
Liver Cake Recipe

Ingredients

2 1b flour
2 lb liver
2 eggs
head of garlic
milk if necessary to blend

Method

Liquidise the liver and garlic.
Then blend all of the ingredients together.
Line a baking tin (may need more than one depending on size).
Pour mixture into tin approx. 1/2" thick.
Bake until set (190° Gas mark 4)
Approx. 1/2 hour
Cool
Cut into titbit size pieces
Freeze in suitable portions
Defrost before use.

More Books By Angela White

Everybody Can Train Their Own Dog,

A - Z of Dog training and behaviour problems for all dogs owners. Endorsed by a founder member of the British Institute of Professional Dog Trainers, and with the ASPCA seal of approval, this easy to follow book gives advice in a handy, fully illustrated format. A must for every dog owner.
Published 1992 TFH
ISBN 0-86622-524-2
Price £10.95 Plus £2.50 P&P UK (£3.50 P&P rest of the world)

Happy Dogs Happy Winners

Complete manual of obedience training. Endorsed by top obedience champion handlers, this book is ideal for complete beginners and more experienced handlers alike. Each exercise is covered with a step by step approach to enable the discerning trainer to work their way from the beginner class right through to championship level competition.
First published 1993 Rainbow Publishing,
ISBN 1-899057-00-5
Price £10.95 inc. P&P UK, (Plus £2.90 P&P rest of the world).
Also available in German Translation Price £13.50 Plus P&P as above.

Puppies Your Successful Guide To Dog Ownership

This definitive work covers every aspect of puppy care right through to adulthood. How to chose a pet, how to look after it, why it behaves in the way it does, how to train it and much more. This book is not just for new puppy owners but, is an ideal book for all who have an interest in dogs.
Published 1997 UK, TFH/Kingdom
ISBN 185279023-7
Price £19.95 Plus £3.00 P&P UK (£4.50 rest of the world)

The Leonberger

Essential reading for anyone interested in this most majestic of breeds. This spell-binding, beautifully illustrated book includes the fascinating history of the breed, how to train using kind, humane, motivational methods, and even the breeding of this giant of the dog world. It is most definitely a user's guide to owning the most magnificent of breeds, the Leonberger.

Published 1998, TFH/Kingdom ISBN 185279064-4
Price £24.95 Plus £3.00 P&P UK (£4.50 rest of the world)

Booklets

Ideal for own use of resale in dog class

Clicker and Target Training - Teaching for fun and competition

An explanation of what clicker training is all about. Step by step advice on how to condition your dog to a clicker and progressing to target training. This informative booklet explains how to use the system to compliment your current training routines or as a complete training concept.

How To Be Top Dog

How to recognise, deal with and treat dominant dogs in a domestic environment. From simple growls to vicious attacks, this booklet helps owners avoid confrontations and get the behaviour under their own control.

Home Alone Canine

Getting dogs used to being alone. How to combat stress, and the problems owners face when they leave their dogs alone. Including chewing, barking, urinating and defecating as well as other associated behaviours.

Training Your Pet Dog

Basic techniques for getting control of your pet. All based on kind methods that work with the dog's own desires. Sit, down, stand, come back, walk on a loose lead, leave when told and don't jump up.

Second Hand Dogs

The special needs of dogs who have been rescued, found wandering or simply rehomed for other reasons. Covers abuse, neglect, confusion, rehabilitation and much more.

He's Not Stupid He's Deaf

Many handlers have to deal with deafness when they get a pup or as the animal grows older. How to recognise and test for deafness, how to deal with and train dogs who are deaf. This booklet also covers teaching dogs who are blind or partially sighted.

Not On The Carpet!

Teach your dog where to urinate and defecate and get it on command. Ideal for new dog owners or owners having problems in house training their dogs. Different ideas and advice for a variety of homes and circumstances.

Booklets all published by Rainbow, 2000.
£3.99 Plus 50p P&P UK
(£1.00 P&P Europe, £1.50 P&P rest of the world)
Order 10 or more copies 10% discount

All above books and booklets available direct from address below: Signed copies available. Please state any message required in block capitals.

More copies of this book '**The Dog Training Instructor's Manual**' also available price £12.95 inc P&P UK (Plus £2.90 P&P rest of the world).

Club and trade enquiries welcome.

Rainbow, PO Box 1044, Haxey, Doncaster. DN9 2JL
Telephone/Fax: 01427 753918 (24 hour ansaphone service)
E.mail IABTC@tinyonline.co.uk
Visit our web site: www.iabtc.co.uk

Please make cheques payable to 'Rainbow'.

International Animal Behaviour Training Centre

Near Doncaster, South Yorkshire, England.
with Course Leader Angela White

Courses available include:

Instructing Pet Owners• - Learn up to date motivational techniques and the art of successful teaching both in classes and one to one. New and would be instructors and those with more experience learn together to create an informal and most informative atmosphere. Graduated certificates available, depending on level achieved.

Behaviour Problems - Learn how to analyse and deal with problem behaviours in dogs.

Canine Behavioural Problem Counselling• - Designed for those who have already achieved a reasonable level of canine behaviour and training knowledge, can already instruct and are interested in or are already counselling dog owners. To develop counselling and diagnostic skills, explore a range of cases, analyse modifications and results.

Feline Behavioural Problem Counselling• - Designed for those who have already achieved a reasonable level of knowledge and ability to handle and are interested in or are already counselling cat owners. To develop counselling and diagnostic skills, explore a range of cases, analyse modifications and results.

Rehabilitating Rescues - Maximise potential new homes by working through problem behaviours and helping new owners to make the adjustments.

Ultimate Dog Training Holiday - Angela White and John Barron are course leaders offering you 5 days of Obedience, Working Trials, Flyball and Agility. Try everything or select your favourite areas. Tuition given on all sports.

Competitive Obedience - If you enjoyed reading Happy Dogs Happy Winners you will love these courses. To suit all levels from beginner to C, working together in harmony. FCI and other country's variations also covered where appropriate.

Obedience Training Holiday - Competitive Obedience - 5 days holiday with your dogs, with structured training sessions every day, mock show, ring set up. Come and have a break with your dog(s) and enjoy some quality training too. Also - just for fun - agility, flyball, tracking. Tents/caravans/motor homes welcome on site or local B&B available (book early). Peaceful country and woodland setting. Families welcome - (participating or not)

Working Trials Weekend - With guest instructor John Barron. Teaching to all levels, beginner and more advanced. Tracking, searching, agility and control.

Training For The Media - Learn what is needed to prepare your dog for film and TV work.

Clicker Training - Learn the art of clicker training, understand its uses, and have fun shaping behaviours for all aspects of training and behaviour control.

Also

Private Tuition - One to one or small group teaching is available on all of the above areas by appointment.

Correspondence Courses• - Open learning in the comfort of your own home and at your own pace. A wide variety of courses to study, full back up given, qualified tutor support.

• = (I.A.B.T.C. certificates of qualification available on these courses). Certificate of attendance available for all courses

For more details on individual courses plus dates, prices and booking forms send stamped addressed envelope to the address below.

Course and IABTC leader Angela White can also be booked to teach at your own venue in the UK and world-wide. Courses can be structured to meet your needs on training, behaviour and many other areas of animal care.

Contact: **Angela or Michael White**,
PO Box 1044, Haxey, Doncaster. DN9 2JN.
Telephone/Fax: 01427 753918 (24 hour ansaphone)
email IABTC@tinyonline.co.uk
or visit our web site www.iabtc.co.uk

Suggested Reference, Reading and Viewing

Here are just a few titles to whet your appetite, the more you read the more you learn, so don't stop here. All titles are books unless otherwise stated.

DOG BEHAVIOUR , PSYCHOLOGY & TRAINING

The Dogs Mind, Bruce Fogle (Pelham), 1990
Games Pets Play, Bruce Fogle (Collins), UK, 1983
The Behaviour of Dogs, Wolves and Related Canids, Michael Fox, (Jonathon Cape), UK, 1971
How Animals Communicate, M W Fox and J A Cohen, (Indiana Univeristy Press), 1977
Dog Behaviour, Dr Ian Dunbar (TFH), 1979
Man Meets Dog, Konrad Lorenz (Methuen)
On Aggression, Konrad Lorenz (Methuen), UK, 1966
Animal Play Behaviour, Robert Fagan, (Oxford University Press), 1981
In Tune With Your Dog, John Rogerson. (Originally published as Your Dog, Popular Dogs Publishing 1988) Revised edition published 1997 UK (Northern Centre for Animal Behaviour).
The New Knowledge of Dog Behaviour, Clarence Pfaffenberger (Howell), USA.
Dog Psychology, Whitney (Howell), USA
On Behaviour, Karen Pryor (Sunshine Books), USA, 1995
Lads Before the Wind, Karen Pryor (Sunshine Books), USA, 1975
Don't Shoot The Dog, Karen Pryor (Bantam Books), USA, 1985
Behaviour Sampler, Gary Wilks (C&T Publishing), USA, 1994
Puppies, Your Guide to Successful Ownership, Angela White (TFH/Kindom) UK, 1997, ISBN 185279023-7
Problem Dog, Behaviour and Misbehaviour, Valerie O'Farrell, UK 1989 (Methuen)
Dog's Best Friend, How Not To Be A Problem Owner, Valerie O'Farrell, UK 1994 (Methuen)
Everybody Can Train Their Own Dog, Angela White, (TFH) ISBN 0-86622-524-2

The Domestic Dog, its evolution, behaviour and interactions with people, edited by James Serpell, UK,1995 (Cambridge University Press)
Open and Utility Training, The Motivational Method, Jack and Wendy Volhard, (Howell) USA, 1992.
How To House Break Your Dog in 7 Days, Shirlee Kaistone, Published USA, 1985, (Bantam Books)
Genetics and the Social Behaviour of the Dog, Scott and Fuller, University of Chicargo Press, USA, 1965.
Dog Training For Children, Video - Dr Ian Dunbar, (James & Kenneth)

PUPPY TRAINING

Puppies, Your Guide to Successful Ownership, Angela White (TFH/Kindom books), UK, 1997 ISBN 185279023-7
Perfect Puppy, Gwen Bailey (Hamlyn), UK, 1995
Sirius Puppy Training Video, Dr Ian Dunbar (James & Kenneth)

NUTRITION , HEALTH CARE & THERAPIES

The Holistic Guide to a Heathy Dog, Wendy Volhard & Kerry Brown, DVM (Howell)
The Work of Dr Edward Bach,
An Introduction and Guide to the 38 Flower Remedies, (Wigmore Publications Ltd), UK, 1995
Dogs: Homeopathic Remedies, George Macleod, (Daniel), UK, Revised 1992.
The Tellington Touch, Linda Tellington-Jones.
The Waltham book of Companion Animal Nutrition, Edney (Pergamon)
Veterinary Notes for Dog Owners, Turner
Water, Your Bodies Many Cries For, Dr F Batmanghelidj, second revised edition published 1997 UK (The Therapist Ltd)

INSTRUCTING AND TEACHING PRACTICE

Teaching Training and Learning, Ian Reece and Stephen Walker, third edition published 1997 UK (Business Education Publishers Ltd.)
How to Communicate Effectively, Bert Decker, 1995 UK (Kogan Page Ltd)
Teaching Dog Obedience Classes, Joachim Volhard & Gail Fisher, 1986 USA (Howell)
Evans Guide For Counselling Dog Owners, Job Michael Evans, USA, 1984 (Howell)
Dictionary of Canine Terms, Frank Jackson, UK, 1995 (Crowood Press)